THE FEW. THE PROUD.

THE FEW. THE PROUD.

WOMEN MARINES IN HARM'S WAY

Sara Sheldon

Foreword by Tracy L. Garrett

PRAEGER SECURITY INTERNATIONAL
Westport, Connecticut • London

Library of Congress Cataloging-in-Publication Data

Sheldon, Sara.
   The few, the proud : women marines in harm's way / Sara Sheldon.
     p. cm.
   Includes bibliographical references and index.
   ISBN-13: 978–0–275–99993–3 (alk. paper)
1. United States. Marine Corps—Women. 2. Women soldiers. I. Title.
UB416.W65 S44 2008
956.7044′345092273—dc22   2007032880

British Library Cataloguing in Publication Data is available.

Library of Congress Catalog Card Number: 2007032880
ISBN-13: 978–0–275–99993–3

First published in 2008

Praeger Security International, 88 Post Road West, Westport, CT 06881
An imprint of Greenwood Publishing Group, Inc.
www.praeger.com

Printed in the United States of America

The paper used in this book complies with the
Permanent Paper Standard issued by the National
Information Standards Organization (Z39.48–1984).

10 9 8 7 6 5 4 3 2 1

Copyright Acknowledgment

The author and publisher gratefully acknowledge permission for use of the following
material:

An Open Letter to Marines of Communications Company, by Capt Amy Alger, © 2005. Reprinted
with permission of Capt Alger.

To all the United States Marines who happen to be women, and to my son, Edward P. Olson

CONTENTS

A photo essay section follows page 74.

FOREWORD

I met Sara Sheldon briefly, days before departing from my assignment in Iraq. She was tucked in a corner at a makeshift plywood desk in the public affairs office in our small headquarters. The window openings of the room were filled with carefully stacked sandbags with heavy blast curtains hung over them. The roof and walls of the building were a foot thick and made of reinforced concrete. Next to the building was a dirty, noisy generator, daily serviced by a patient Marine sergeant and refueled by an Iraqi contractor. The tanker of fuel made its way out to our headquarters each day through a labyrinth of security gates, guards, and checkpoints—a rolling explosive device, capable of leveling our building and killing everyone in it. The headquarters was on the edge of a large airfield, in constant use, day and night, shuttling personnel, supplies, and equipment to and through Al Anbar province. The Muj, as we called them, often targeted the headquarters, and shrapnel from frequent rocket attacks left deep pock marks on the outside walls and doors, and cracked the windows. Our camp, housing thousands of service members, contractors, and international workers, constituted a "rear area," a term woefully misused in descriptions of the current nonlinear battle space. Outside the gate, on the other side of the perimeter fence, beyond the view of the sentries, was the close fight, and daily we felt its effects in roadside bombs, small-arms fire, mortars, and rockets.

Most media representatives during my tour were anxious to experience the war up close. They wanted to get out on patrol, shadowing the infantry units and reporting on the clash of Al Qaeda and Coalition forces. Helicopter rides to forward positions were popular, but that was before we started losing so many. Few reporters wanted to endure the ten-hour night convoy around the lake to Fallujah and back or to cover the daily slog of searching Iraqis at checkpoints inside the city. The potato factory that we used as a temporary storage and processing station for the remains of Iraqi insurgents killed during a major operation in Fallujah was not on their itinerary either. I did not meet a single reporter at the tent camp we set up inside our perimeter for Iraqis who had volunteered to serve as polling station workers during the January 2005 elections. There just was not much interest in the mundane chores of combat support.

Women, though, are attentive to the quotidian. We always have been. So, perhaps it takes a woman to tell the stories of women in war in a manner that rings true. Sara's patience to seek out the mail clerks, administrators, disbursers, intelligence analysts, food service supervisors, public affairs officers, radio operators, drivers, and MPs was rewarded. Using the peripheral vision of a gatherer, she took it all in. With one story in hand, she would be led to another female Marine. It was almost an Underground Railroad kind of environment; women knew where other women were in the 40,000-person force. She was passed from one to another like a precious object, not to be hoarded or kept secret or buried in one place, but connected to others in order to further the connection.

For over 200 years, the American public has perpetuated the mythology of the Marine Corps. Kernels of truth have been layered over with feelings and impressions and memories until you can hardly see where it all began. Some part is always obscured. It is an altruistic collection of stories with both valiant heroes and dreadful scoundrels.

Once you join the Marine Corps, the intangible reasons you were drawn to it become visible to you. My dad was a Marine, and I essentially joined the Corps when I was a high school senior and was accepted into the Navy ROTC program at our state university, with a Marine Option. Initially, I would have said that I joined because I needed the support to get a college education. After leaving active duty, I always thought I joined the Reserves so that I could continue to contribute to our family finances while being a full-time mom. But somewhere along the way, it stopped being a vehicle for me to get something and became the way I *served.* My service has always required discipline and dedication to high ideals; I am both challenged and charged with challenging those who work for me to be ready warriors.

In the Marine Corps, we make quite a bit of the formidable experience of the Crucible, a part of boot camp training that teaches recruits, through hardship, the values of personal responsibility and team spirit. Once through the Crucible, a recruit is given the Eagle, Globe, and Anchor, our emblem, and for the first time, he or she is called "Marine." Henceforth, each Marine will have a new lens through which to see himself or herself and others. He or she has known what is tough, nearly beyond enduring, and recognizes that it is only through the support and encouragement of his or her fellows that he or she is able to meet the mission.

Much has been made of the potentially negative effect on men of having women in the combat zone. But my experience was that Marines saw only other Marines wherever they looked. Could you do the job? Could you pull your weight? Nonhackers come in both genders, all races, and every occupational specialty. You put that million dollars of cash in your ALICE pack and travel through the Iraqi night to deliver it to commanders in the field who need to pay their contractors—that is all that is asked of you. You get the media representatives to Fallujah or Balad safely and you have done your job. You search under the abaya of every indignant Iraqi wife or mother coming to the food distribution site and you will keep your fellows alive to fight and serve another day. And in the process, if you get shot at or an IED detonates under your vehicle, or a suicide bomber chooses your shift to die for his or her cause, it is a chance you are willing to take, to be a Marine and serve some higher purpose that even you cannot define very well.

Read the stories of these daughters of Athena and glimpse the strength and devotion of each one of them. They are outside of cliché—they do not have chips on their shoulders about equality between the sexes, and they have probably never debated the issue of women in combat. These women want the challenge and the change that the Marine Corps promises to all who join. Marching to the sound of the guns is not an option for them; it is a moral obligation. In the words of our service oath, they take it freely, without any mental reservation or purpose of evasion. Most Marines, men and women alike, are not looking to be heroes of any kind; they just want to be Marines.

I did not have much time to talk with Sara the day we met. I was transitioning my duties to those on the new team coming in to relieve us. She was a loose end that needed tying up. Was she going to be on the flight out that night? Yes, Capt Amy Malugani, our Public Affairs Officer, would see to that. Was there anything more we could do for her before she left? No, she was fine. She was taking advantage of the relative warmth and safety of our headquarters to work on her notes. "Glad we could help," I said. "That's what we are here for."

Tracy L. Garrett
Brigadier General
United States Marine Corps

PREFACE

How did I get to Iraq? It is a common question, and a reasonable one, since I am not a working journalist, not in the military, and was, at the time I embedded, 70 years old.

I have long been intrigued with the why of things—mostly chunks of history that have been explained inadequately in books or in the media, igniting my curiosity. I am a research hound, constantly reading biography and history and poring over maps. There are so many unexplained irregularities that I long to resolve.

I never give up. Areas of intense interest follow me forever, and I may veer back to pick them up long after I have moved to another subject. When I was young, I was very interested in China—the long chronicle of dynasties, the esoteric art, architecture, and music. The language fascinated me. During my high school years, China was "lost" to communism, and the news media presented what I thought was a very one-sided story of that historical event. McCarthyism marginalized any further inquiry, and my plan to go into Chinese studies at university was greatly discouraged.

After college, I made a career in arts administration in which I still work today, as associate director of the Leanin' Tree Museum and Sculpture Garden of Western Art. I spent several years in Santa Fe where I founded and directed the now-defunct Santa Fe Festival of the Arts. Because of the distracting and never-ending debate over the aesthetics of modern vs. traditional art that prevails in the art world, I lost interest in the visual arts and decided to go to graduate school in, of course, Chinese studies. President Richard M. Nixon had made China a hot topic by then.

After graduate school I began research on a biography of Pan Yuliang, a woman painter in the Chinese modern art movement. In China to research her early life, I found that because of long years of the communist persecution of intellectuals and the systematic destruction of scholarship, I was stonewalled. There were few facts known about her, but endless undocumented stories and fictional narratives. The material I needed from the years preceding Mao Zedong's People's Republic in 1949 was unavailable to me for "reasons of state security."

In 1991, while traveling in China, I called home to check in and was surprised when my son asked me to sit down because he had something to tell me. He had joined the Marine Corps. He was correct that it would come as a total surprise to me. I knew very little about the military and had not known he was thinking of enlisting. I did not understand how the Marine Corps could take precedence over any number of other options he had in his life. A gifted student, he chose to do this after completing two years of university and without taking advantage of officer training. He enlisted as an infantryman. In trying to explain his decision, he stimulated in me what has become an ongoing interest in why people choose service in the military.

While following his transformation into a Marine, I gained new insight into the pride and professionalism of this branch of the military. My perception was exponentially expanded, and I had a new "why" to explore. My son told me that the 1/4 Marines (his unit—1st Battalion, 4th Regiment) had a history of being deployed in China prior to World War II. It was the very period of my area of study—the time of the "loss" of China.

I toyed with the idea of writing a novel about the Marine Corps to put my new information to use and to try to grasp why it fascinated me so. My son discouraged me, citing my lack of knowledge of all things military. I contacted the Marines, worked with very constructive advisors in every area of warfare, and in 1998 the novel *Operation Restore America* was published. I wrote a sequel, another novel, *Capitol Terror,* about a terrorist attack in Washington, D.C., which failed to find a publisher because it was considered implausible. After 9/11 *Capitol Terror* appeared very plausible indeed, but tame in comparison with the attack on the World Trade Center. There was an unspoken moratorium on terrorist fiction, TV, and movies for about a year, and by then I was more interested in the coming war in Iraq and the fact that the Marine advisors whom I had come to know well, many of them women, were being deployed to a combat zone.

I dug into the politics of the war and in no time I became a news junkie. A writer loves on-site research to capture the flavor and everyday detail needed to flesh out a book, but going to Iraq seemed a little over the top. I thought that with Google Earth, the infinite number of military facts available on the Internet, plus my daily contact with Marines in Iraq, I could produce a credible nonfiction work about women Marines in the war zone.

Then came the e-mail from Col Jenny Holbert that changed everything. I have known Col Holbert for a dozen years, beginning with my participation, as a media observer, in the Marines' Urban Warrior operations in the mid-1990s when I was researching CBIRF, the Marine Corps Chemical Biological Incident Response Force.

"Why don't you come and see for yourself?" was her response to a surfeit of queries from me by e-mail when she deployed to Iraq. I had sent her questions asking how many women Marines were deployed and to what jobs they were assigned. Were they in combat? If not allowed in combat, then how could they avoid combat since all of Iraq had quickly become a volatile war zone?

Once again I was confused by what I knew, by now, about Marines, and what the media was saying about the war. It could not be all shock and awe or IEDs. How were we getting food and water to the troops? Where were they billeted? What about the thousands of tons of war materiel I heard was being shipped to Iraq, and the enormous number of support troops for the infantrymen—the huge bases being supplied and managed? What sort of phenomenal logistics did that take? Knowing that it takes about seven Marines working inside the wire to put every Marine rifleman outside the wire, I was frustrated at the lack of information available about the everyday operational detail. I felt I had to go see for myself. Col Holbert informed me that as a writer, I could embed with the Marines at Camp Fallujah. She was enthusiastic about having another legitimate observer and storyteller in the Area of Operation to expand the viewpoint of the people back home about Operation Iraqi Freedom.

I was not sure Col Holbert's invitation was serious. I joked about it when I told my two daughters about the possibility of my going to Iraq. But when I told my son, now a retired Marine with a family, he said, "When are you going?" I was struck dumb. He continued, "How many people get invited to go to Iraq? This is a tremendous opportunity, Mom. You'll regret it if you don't go." How many people WANT an invitation to Iraq, I wondered. But the idea was implanted, the die was cast. I went.

ACKNOWLEDGMENTS

I want to acknowledge the gracious accommodation and assistance with my journey to Iraq to research this book given me by Ed and Tom Trumble, of Leanin' Tree, Inc. Col Holbert spent hours going over the manuscript to edit it according to USMC protocol, and LtGen Carol Mutter, USMC (ret.), also made valuable comments. Also, my thanks go to Sandy Adler for her professional work of transcribing the taped interviews from Iraq, some of which were almost inaudible because of the noise of generators. Thomas Howard edited the photos I took under severe conditions of harsh sunlight and deep shadows, and Gordon Keiser kept me honest. And I am grateful for the enthusiasm and encouragement of Paula Sarlls, president of the Women Marines Association, and Nancy Wilt, VP of the Colorado Chapter of WMA. To all the Marines I met in Iraq who shouldered my pack, shared their stories with me, and facilitated my journey—Oorah!

ACRONYMS

NOTE: All time is referred to as military time, using a 24-hour clock: 0000–2400.

ALICE   All-purpose, Lightweight, Individual Carrying Equipment—a pack

AO   Area of Operation

ASVAB   Armed Services Vocational Aptitude Battery test

BFT   Blue Force Tracker, a navigation and tracking system

BIAP   Baghdad International Airport

C-130   Large tactical Air Force cargo plane

CAG   Civil Affairs Group, working with civil authorities and populations

CH-46   Boeing tandem-rotor assault helicopter

CMOC   Civil-Military Operations Center

CO   Commanding Officer

COC   Combat Operations Center

CPIC   Coalition Press Information Center

DHL   International air express company

DoD   Department of Defense

DSN   Defense Switched Network of telephones

ECP   Entry Control Point

EPW   Enemy Prisoner of War

FIOCA   Female Information and Operations Civil Affairs

FSF   Female Search Force

G.I.   Abbreviation for Government Issue, and nickname for military personnel

GPS	Global Positioning System
IED	Improvised Explosive Device
I-MEF	1st Marine Expeditionary Force
II-MEF	2nd Marine Expeditionary Force
IP	Iraqi Police
IR	Infrared
IRR	Inactive Regular Reserve
IZ	International Zone (in Baghdad)
K9	Military designation for war dogs (canine)
KBR	Kellogg, Brown and Root, a subsidiary of Halliburton
M9	9mm (millimeter) military pistol
M16	U.S. rifle, caliber—5.56mm
MASH	Military Army Surgical Hospital
MCRD	Marine Corps Recruit Depot—training base for Marine recruits
MCT	Marine Combat Training
MEK	Mujahideen-e-Khalq, a militant Iranian antigovernment group
MOPP	Mission Oriented Protective Posture—chemical/biological suits
MOS	Military Occupational Specialty
MP	Military Police
MRE	Meal Ready-to-Eat
NBC	Nuclear/Biological/Chemical
NCO	Non-Commissioned Officer
NVG	Night Vision Goggles
OIC	Officer In Charge
OIF	Operation Iraqi Freedom—the Iraqi War
OCS	Officer Candidates School
PAO	Public Affairs Office
PC	Personal Computer
PFC	Private First Class
PRC-119	Portable Radio Case-119
PTSD	Post-Traumatic Stress Disorder

PX   Post Exchange, a store at a military installation

QRF   Quick Reaction Force

RCT-1   Regimental Combat Team-1

RIP   Relief In Place, replacement of troops

ROE   Rules of Engagement

ROTC   Reserve Officer Training Corps

R&R   Rest and Relaxation

RTCH   Rough Terrain Container Handlers

TBS   The Basic School

TCN   Third-Country National

TQ   Taqqadum

USAID   U.S. Agency for International Development

USDA   U.S. Department of Agriculture

VIP   Very Important Person

XO   Executive Officer

1

ARRIVING IN IRAQ

"You can spot a Marine a mile away," says the KBR independent contractor who serves as *concierge* at the Army's Camp Striker at Baghdad International Airport, where I spend my first night in Iraq. "It's the way they carry themselves."

Right. But then I ask her, "Can you tell a woman Marine from a guy?"

Silence. Then, "I never noticed one way or the other."

In identical uniforms and wearing full body armor, Marines look the same, regardless of gender. Many Americans do not know that women serve as United States Marines. And if they do, they usually assume the women are secretaries, drivers, clerks, or food service workers. And they assume that if these women Marines are in Iraq, they are not in any danger. As more casualties involve women Marines, the awareness of the public is being raised, and many are curious as to what, exactly, they do in Iraq.

In February 2005, two weeks after the Iraqi national elections, I traveled alone to Iraq to embed with the 1st Marine Expeditionary Force at Camp Fallujah to interview women Marines. At 70, this was an extreme adventure for me. As a freelance writer, I did not have a media employer paying my way. I secured my own airline ticket to Kuwait, and body armor (a state-of-the-art flak jacket with ceramic plates, rented on the Internet), Kevlar helmet, and combat boots, and then worked out in the gear for three weeks prior to my departure.

My mission was to interview women Marines, from corporals to colonels, in all Military Occupational Specialties. The Marine Public Affairs officer for Iraq, Col Jenny Holbert, who had dealt with my request to embed, put me in touch with the Army at the Coalition Press Information Center (CPIC) in Baghdad. The Army handles all arrangements for civilians visiting Iraq.

I e-mailed CPIC to begin the procedures to embed. I am a writer, not a journalist—a different breed altogether. I did not intend to accompany

Marine infantry units on raids or patrols into cities, as a reporter. I was interested in interviewing women Marines about their work in Iraq. I would be on the Marine bases, not in dangerous areas.

That, I learned soon enough, was an entirely naïve assumption. Again, most Americans know little about the details of our presence in Iraq. They believe that we occupy the country, in the sense of "to take and hold possession of" according to the definition. One thinks of the occupation of Japan after World War II, when the United States became *ipso facto* the government of the country and was responsible for all transportation, utilities, supply, facilities, and the economy of the country as it rebuilt. Iraq is not the same. The United States occupies many very large military bases throughout Iraq; beyond that it has no control whatsoever. It has influence, of course, by dint of its power. Because the Coalition Government has called the shots from Baghdad since Saddam Hussein was ousted, U.S. troops have occupied only the small International Zone (the IZ, also called the Green Zone) of the city. Beyond that, their fiat was, and is, challenged everywhere. Recently, the IZ has proven increasingly vulnerable to attack and even the elected Iraqi government is at risk.

The American public has probably realized by now that the IZ is a fortress more than a secure center of command and control. Step outside the IZ or go "outside the wire" of the military bases and Coalition forces are not in control. The roads between bases and throughout the country, as well as the entire airspace, are extremely dangerous. We can be said to "own" the airspace, in the sense that no enemy aircraft fly there, but we are not safe there. All American and Coalition aircraft are subject to attack from the ground at any time.

For almost two years, most notorious was the short, seven-mile stretch of highway known as Route Irish between the edge of Baghdad and the Baghdad International Airport (BIAP), which was struck frequently by suicide bombers, insurgents with mortars, or IEDs (Improvised Explosive Devices). During that period there were on average 94 attacks by insurgents every day in Iraq, whose area compares roughly to the size of California. Of those, one-third occurred in Baghdad, with one or two every day on Route Irish. That short span is traveled daily, of necessity, by every VIP and civilian entering or leaving the country to pick up press credentials or meet their work supervisors or the Iraqi government and top American military commanders. It is a freeway like any other highway to a major airport in the United States or any country, except that it is entirely beyond our ability to secure it. More recently, with newly trained Iraqi forces in control of the road, the number of attacks has decreased.

The highway runs through typical suburban areas, with three major interchanges ringed at places with areas of multistoried apartment buildings, dilapidated commercial areas, or ordinary neighborhoods. Any of the buildings along the highway allow for easy surveillance by insurgents of schedules of transport and can serve as places to build IEDs or from which to fire on vehicles using the road. There are not enough troops to clear and then occupy the areas bordering the road on that seven-mile stretch. All roads in Iraq are subject to this danger.

Helicopters travel back and forth from BIAP to the IZ, most often at night, 200 to 250 feet off the ground. Iraq is mostly dark, and the military prefers it that way. The larger cities have electricity for varying times during the day and night, but the countryside and flight lines at all the military bases are black. Helicopters are extremely loud, especially just barely above the deck, but they are virtually impossible to see when they move so quickly at such low altitudes. Before you can follow the sound and actually catch a glimpse of them, they are gone. The low altitude makes it difficult to take accurate aim at them from the ground. They often fly in pairs or threes, and once they leave their secure base, they fly their routes, their arrival announced only minutes before they touch down, and they never turn off their engines or turn on their lights. They fly with infrared and blackout instruments, which give a ghoulish green glow to the cockpits. Gunners ride in open doorways on either side, behind the pilot and the copilot, scanning the ground through their night vision goggles with their 7.62mm machine guns.

Military personnel travel this way as a matter of course; civilian passengers are extraneous cargo on a very dangerous flight schedule. The Army is tasked with providing transport for civilians and does it on a space-available basis. It is possible to rent vehicles and drivers to travel privately, but the dangers are much greater because the Army has no information as to your whereabouts and the rescue possibilities are just about nil in case of attack.

C-130 Hercules cargo planes, with turboprop engines, capable of carrying 42,000 pounds at 350 miles per hour, do some of the ferrying of troops into and around Iraq. The flight from Kuwait to Baghdad International Airport is knee-to-knee in an open cargo bay in which an average of 40 passengers is dwarfed by palettes of supplies, from K9 dogs to front-end loaders. It is crowded and loud even with ear plugs, and the final approach down to the runway at BIAP from 15,000 or 20,000 feet is a corkscrew maneuver to foil whatever unfriendly attack may be afoot. Frequent fliers on that route use a variety of wristbands, ear clips, and medications to survive the stomach-churning plunge.

When I left the Marriott Hotel in Kuwait City I took two apples from the complimentary bowl of fruit in my room—which turned out to be a good thing.

Landing at BIAP when I come off the C-130 from Kuwait, I stand in the middle of the enormous airfield, watching people scatter in all directions.

I am told there is no transportation to Baghdad that day, no helicopters flying, no Rhino buses driving—I have no idea what to do. The manifest officer has no answers for me other than for me to go to the terminal and ask my questions there. He points vaguely across the field.

Where is the terminal? There are no signs, and there is no general exodus in any one direction, so I cannot follow the crowd. Everyone, it seems, is being met or knows where he or she is going. I am the outsider. I ask several people to point out the terminal. Soldiers have not a clue—they just follow their orders—wait here, go there, line up. Contractors are mostly met by coworkers and head for their company vehicles in the parking lot. Finally an Army captain points to a line of shacks: I go into one after another, backing out of each when it appears to be the wrong one, getting more amused at the double-takes as soldiers look at me—definitely an outsider—an older, white-haired woman alone, in armor and combat boots and carrying a helmet and a pack.

When I finally find the terminal, I ask an Air Force sergeant if I can make a phone call. I have phone numbers for everybody—the Army officers with whom I am to meet at the press center in Baghdad, as well as Col Holbert and her media officer, Lt Gilbert. The sergeant points at the heavy, black 1950s-type phone on the plywood counter. I pick it up—nothing, no dial tone. "Just dial," she says. "And wait. It may take awhile." I dial and there is no sound of ringing, but I wait. After a couple of minutes, the sergeant looks over and says, "Try it again." So I do, and after a long, anxious minute or two I hear the familiar military surge of introduction: "Lieutenantgilbertpublicaffairscampfallujah." I have a rush of assurance—even more so when he tells me they had been waiting for my call.

The DSN (Defense Switched Network) telephones in Iraq are available only to the military. The calls on DSN are placed as a connection becomes available. If there is no connection available, a computer scans the calls to see which has a higher preference—the waiting call or one in place. If the waiting call has preference, the call in place is terminated and the line goes dead. Calls on DSN are necessarily short. There are cell phones on the commercial network called Iraqna. Most of the enlisted military have no reason to use either. AT&T phone centers on the bases have telephones for calls to the States for use by the military with phone cards or with cash. They are generally open 24 hours a day and are staffed by contractors. The media uses satellite phones, as do many military offices. The cell phones and DSN are subject to interruption of service, as the relay towers are often put out of service by the military. This happened frequently when IEDs were being detonated remotely by cell phones. Now the insurgents have gotten more sophisticated and can use timers for clothes dryers, walkie-talkies, and radios as detonation devices.

Being without a cell phone, or any ready means of communication, is daunting when you are alone in a foreign setting and unaware of how to get to your destination—even where it is, and how far. We are such a connected society. In Iraq, you cannot just rent a car at the airport, or buy a ticket for a bus or train. You cannot go online to MapQuest or call a taxi. You have no idea how you will get to where you are supposed to be. That is the job of the military.

After I speak to Lt Gilbert, who tells me I will have to find accommodations somewhere for the night and sign up for a flight or bus ride into Baghdad in the morning, I am once again reliant on the Air Force sergeant. She points to a sign on the wall that says "Camp Striker—The Stables." I call and am told to get on the bus and come over—there is a space for me.

Where is the bus? "In the parking lot. It runs every half hour," the sergeant tells me. In the parking lot there are half a dozen buses parked headed in various directions with their doors open and empty. I wait until I see three civilians (maybe contractors? I have no idea) who look like they might be waiting for the bus to Camp Striker, and I ask. Sure enough. So I wait with them. The bus that arrives is an ancient Iraqi bus with a sign in the window that has the destination in Arabic.

"How do you know this is the right bus?" I ask the contractor.

"I've taken it before." He helps me load my pack in the luggage compartment, and we ride to Camp Striker. At the wooden gazebo erected as a bus stop at the camp, we disembark and I go in the direction the contractor points to find the office of the "concierge."

The concierge is another contractor, a good-natured, self-assured Hawaiian policewoman, who looks at my name when I sign in and says, "You've had two telephone calls. Are you with the State Department?"

That is how I learn that phone usage in Iraq is rare. Nobody gets phone calls in Iraq on DSN who is not in the military or a VIP. It takes me 30 minutes to get a call through on her DSN line, but it is lovely to know that Lt Gilbert is checking on me again to make sure I am safe for the night.

"Call me when you get to CPIC," he says. "Have a good journey."

The concierge points out a stack of blankets available for overnight travelers, and I take one and set out in the dark to walk about 200 yards along a row of tents with wooden doors marked "A," "B," "C," etc. until I get to "J." The space inside looks enormous and is unoccupied, so I take the first cot on the left. Portapotties, I had made sure to look for them, are across a 50-foot-wide, dusty driving space. It is 2100 hours and I am too tired to try to find the showers. Notwithstanding the high decibel noise level that is constant in Iraq—from the generators and helicopters, trucks, and planes—I am asleep in minutes.

Without press credentials, which I will get at CPIC in Baghdad, it is next to impossible to eat in the chow halls, so at Camp Striker I go to bed without supper, and the next morning, anxious not to miss being assigned on transport of some kind into Baghdad, I ride the bus back into BIAP at 0600, missing breakfast.

Approaching the checkpoint at BIAP, the bus threads its way through a slalom course of five or six concrete barriers designed to slow everybody down to a crawl. Then there is a sign that reads "THIS IS A KILL ZONE. YOU WILL STOP AT THE SIGN AND PROVIDE 100% ID. YOU WILL NOT PROCEED UNTIL TOLD TO." The bus proceeds and pulls into the crowded parking area at the edge of the military airfield at BIAP, and I head to the passenger terminal in plenty of time—I am the first one there. Transport for civilians, not contractors, into Baghdad, is handled by the American Embassy—a fact I pondered but for which I was never given an explanation. I wait in front of the American Embassy plywood counter, and the manifest clerk for these flights arrives three hours later. It is now 24 hours since I left Kuwait, and I have eaten the last of my apples.

I am manifested on a Black Hawk helicopter to make the flight into Baghdad—during the day, at about 200 feet above ground. Usually helo flights are at night, so I am able to see the city and marvel, yet again, at what I am experiencing.

By now I am able to let go and assume that the Marines will not lose me, and that somewhere, in this vast military bureaucracy, there is a manifest with my name on it for the remainder of my journey. I relinquish all control. After that moment, I never make a decision of my own, except, perhaps, to ask if I can visit a portapotty and where they are located. And I can choose for myself, from the dizzying array of food in the chow hall, what to eat. Beyond that, my hours of rising and retiring, my interviews during the day, the time I go to chow and when and where I sleep, and when and how I move about the country are all out of my control. But, unlike civilian life in the United States, there is someone always looking out for me, tracking my movements, making and revising my schedule —amazing—like an unseen parent. It makes being an outsider insignificant. I am attached to the 1st Marine Expeditionary Force at Camp Fallujah, and I am on a mission. The most memorable words I hear during my trip are, "You're on this flight, ma'am. You're good to go."

The first Marine I encounter, 36 hours after leaving Kuwait, is the gunner of a Humvee who stomps into the passenger terminal at BIAP at 2345 hours, M16 hanging from his shoulder, and a piece of paper in his hand. He looks alert but dusty, with a black hood rolled down around his neck over his cammie uniform. I have recently arrived on a Black Hawk from the IZ where I collected my press credentials at CPIC, and I have been anxious about making the connection with the Marine convoy I am to meet here.

Marines are in charge of Al Anbar province in Iraq—the largest, Western-most area that borders Saudi Arabia, Jordan, and Syria. The rest of Iraq is Army territory. The BIAP facilities are manned by the Army and the Air Force. There is nary a Marine in sight until he arrives. He glances around the terminal (a small building, about 40 feet by 60 feet, that serves 200,000 troops and personnel traveling through BIAP) and immediately zeros in on me. "Sheldon," he says, looking at his paper.

"Yes sir."

"This way." He turns on his heel and heads out. I pick up my computer case and follow him. Outside the door I reach for my backpack leaning against a sign that says "NO BAGS ALLOWED IN TERMINAL." He picks up the pack and throws the 35-pound weight onto his shoulder like a lightweight jacket and leads me along a path through the dark gravel courtyard of lounging soldiers amid the red glow of cigarettes, low cement barriers, pools of mud, past a row of portapotties, and finally into the crowded parking lot with SUVs, pickups, buses, and Humvees parked every which way. The only light comes from a door ajar in a shower trailer and the curtain askew over the doorway of a semi that holds a makeshift PX. He throws the pack on the back of the Humvee and opens the rear door for me. I climb in and squeeze my combat boots into the small space on the floor behind the front seat. He shows me how to shut the door and open it again (it is important to know this) and then goes around to climb up into his gun turret. His feet drop down into the Humvee onto the platform next to my shoulder, two other Marines climb into the front seat, and we are off.

I am relieved. The connection worked and I am with the Marines now, on my way to Camp Fallujah. The officer in front of me begins working with the communications equipment in the front seat—a radio and a satellite phone, GPS, and a monitor with a green, snaking image of the road from the air, several hundred thousand dollars' worth of technology. This is the Blue Force Tracker system used by the military in Iraq, a satellite-based system that allows Marines to use two-way communications beyond line of sight. A dashboard-mounted laptop and a rooftop transponder/receiver beam information via satellite to headquarters and other vehicles. It is a real-time image of the area that shows the Marines where they are and indicates the other vehicles of the convoy. There is a map that can indicate suspected enemy IEDs from information punched in from the Humvee and is instantly available to headquarters, rescue forces, and flights overhead. Thus, everyone shares information on enemy positions. All this I learn later and realize, despite the feeling of our small presence in a very large, dark, dangerous territory, that we are far from alone.

There are metal boxes of ammo next to me on the seat. I glance over at the Marine in the rear seat to my left, on the other side of the gunner's feet, and see that there is a woman. We smile at each other. Then we roar out of the BIAP parking lot and head down a road lined with 12-foot concrete barriers. Finally, there is a curve and then a sign. "THIS IS THE RED ZONE. WEAPONS ARE FREE. LOCK AND LOAD."

There are no longer any barriers, just open desert. The only light is a sliver of rising moon. Through the thick armored-glass window I can make out a few dark shapes of square buildings some distance from the road; once in a while there is a pinprick of light. This is the countryside, this is Iraq.

Immediately, the Marines pull on their helmets and lower their night vision goggles (NVG). The Marines in the front seat check their handguns. The Marine in the back watches me put on my helmet and adjusts her own, putting goggles over her eyes. She has no NVG. I have forgotten to get my goggles out of my backpack.

The officer ahead of me turns and introduces the Marines, talking rapidly, and asks if I have been briefed. No, sir, I tell him. He proceeds in rapid monotone to tell me that if there is an attack and we are fired upon, the vehicle will not stop but will proceed unless disabled. If the Marine next to me goes down, I will feed ammo to the gunner. If the vehicle is disabled, he explains the procedure for exiting the vehicle and taking cover while returning fire (all except for me—I am not allowed to carry a weapon) while we await assistance by the QRF (Quick Reaction Force), which should arrive within minutes. If we are east of Abu Ghraib, the QRF is Army; west, it is the Marines.

Thus begins my adventure with the United States Marines in Iraq.

The Humvees have infrared light beams visible to other drivers on the road. The gunner, sticking through the top of the Hummer, has a small IR "firefly" attached to the back of his helmet that flashes and can be seen from the air to let aircraft overhead know he is a friendly.

I have a chance to talk with the woman Marine beside me when we pause at a KBR (Kellogg, Brown and Root—subsidiary of Halliburton) truck depot to pick up the convoy of semis our Marines are escorting. She tells me her name, but in the din I cannot catch it. She says no one can pronounce it, so they all call her Cpl Kay. That is good enough. She has volunteered to ride along with the three-man Humvee crew to relieve a gunnery sergeant who usually makes the run but was exhausted and run down from fighting a bad cold. Marines looking out for Marines, I think, and then realize that she has, in essence, put herself in a combat situation—a no-no. But the line drawn between combat positions and secure assignments is so faint as to be nearly invisible in Iraq. Also later, I realize that *I* was also in a combat situation, as a passenger. But this is how the military moves visitors about in Iraq—on a space-available basis in whatever vehicle happens to be going to the desired destination. Everyone's name is on a manifest with a date and destination requested. The military makes every effort to comply. The military will supply room, board, and transportation during my tour in country, as well as medical treatment, if needed—a sobering thought.

The convoy we are escorting has as many as 30 semis, driven by Syrians, Americans, Pakistanis, Turks, and others; all highly paid, all employed by KBR. Sometimes the drivers are drunk and create such dangerous havoc that the Marines have to put one of their own men in the cab and carry the driver in the Humvee. This infuriates the Marines, they tell me, as it increases the danger to the convoy, and while they would like to kill the driver, they do not, or torture him. But during the trip they have their fun with him and are pretty sure he will never attempt to drive drunk again.

A short distance along the road I see to my right a long series of bright lights, like a ball field in the distance on a summer night. It is an anomaly in this dark landscape and then it dawns on me—"Is that...?" I start to say to the Major in the seat ahead of me. "Abu Ghraib," he confirms, without turning. My awareness is now complete. Traveling in Iraq is more dangerous than I imagined. I am en route to Camp Fallujah, a Marine base that I assume is relatively secure, via one of the most dangerous highways in Iraq. How else would I get there? By helicopter, perhaps, which I have already discovered, having made two flights out of and back to BIAP, is just as risky. Now I get it.

Later I meet the Marine whose place Cpl Kay took that night—Gunny Morales—and he tells me that these Marine Humvees make this run, the Chow Run, they call it, about three times a week, always at night, escorting semis with supplies for the Marine base. They transport everything from toilet paper to lettuce, body bags to ammunition. Keeping the convoy moving and avoiding any other vehicles cutting into the line of trucks is paramount to security. The line stretches out behind the lead Humvee, and trucks often lag dangerously behind. There is another Marine Humvee traveling midway in the convoy, and another at the end. A "bunny" Humvee travels beside the convoy, dropping back and speeding up to make sure every vehicle is safely in line. To avoid an enemy vehicle slipping into the line, Gunny Morales often devised a way of marking each truck as it passed him at the start of the run—with a playing card, sometimes. Then he dismounted at the gate to Camp Fallujah and collected the cards as the trucks entered, making sure the convoy was complete and unaltered. At the turn into Camp Fallujah, I can finally look back and see the entire convoy following—a long line of trucks it was impossible to view from my armored window.

Gunny Morales also tells me that convoys on the Abu Ghraib road are attacked by gunfire, IEDs, or missiles about three to five times a week. This says a great deal about the courage of the Marines who regularly travel the road, including Cpl Kay, and it is my initiation into the underlying stress of being anywhere in Iraq—in harm's way.

2

WOMEN MARINES—CHOOSING TO BE THE BEST

The first woman Marine served in 1918. Since then, tens of thousands of women have served and pledged themselves to the core values of the Marine Corps: honor, courage, and commitment.

Why do women join the United States Marine Corps? Almost every answer I got was because of the challenge. Like their male counterparts, they want to be the best. But there was never just one reason.

"I'm a Marine down to my core. Everything about me. I would never do anything to violate my personal honor, whatever I'm doing. I try to do what's right. I just carry that with me through my entire life." At 51, Chief Warrant Officer-4 Adamson belies her age—small, wiry, strong, with an overview of the importance of her work in Civil Affairs in Iraq honed from years in law enforcement and the judicial system of the private sector.

When CWO4 Adamson joined the Corps in 1974, she had to write a paper on why the Marine Corps should grant her the privilege of enlisting. There were very few women in the Corps in the early 1970s. She had been in the Army Nursing Corps, hoping to get her degree in nursing so she could join the Army or Navy and be assigned to a MASH unit in Vietnam, the only way, as a woman, she could serve in that war. But the conflict ended before that could happen, so she dropped out of nursing school and joined the Marine Corps, which is where she says she wanted to be in the first place.

Looking down at her field utilities, Adamson says of her first days in the Corps,

> We didn't wear these. We didn't wear combat boots and camouflage utilities. My original uniform issue is in a museum. For physical training we wore powder blue culottes with two big buttons and a powder blue shirt and

white sneakers. Keds. Not running shoes. Keds. We had to use white shoe polish to get the mud off.

We didn't have the same physical fitness tests as they do today. We didn't run as far. We didn't hang on the bars as long. We didn't do sit-ups. And when I was in boot camp, we didn't qualify on the rifle range. We had what they called "Familiarization Class." I remember we got to fire three rounds. We weren't going to be in combat. We're still not in combat. When I go into town, there's a male Marine on the gun and my M16 is just background.

Adamson's Military Occupational Specialty (MOS) is 5805—Criminal Investigation. In 1974, after basic training, she was in air-ground intel, but later applied to change her MOS to 5811, Military Policeman, which would allow her to put in for warrant officer. Adamson lived in Salt Lake City and connected once a month to the Marine Corps Institute, working in counterterrorism and antiterrorism programs. When she was mobilized in 2002 for Operation Iraqi Freedom, she was assigned to Marine Corps Base, Quantico, Virginia, as staff secretary and Antiterrorism Force Protection Officer. Deployed to Iraq in the fall of 2004, she was in Civil Affairs as the Judicial Assessment Officer for Al Anbar province.

Adamson is a Senior Justice Court Judge for Salt Lake County, Utah, and was reelected to that post even though she had been away for two years.

Initially, you're appointed [as judge], and then every four years you run for retention. In 2002, there was an election while I was on active duty at Quantico. When the voter information pamphlet was sent out, it didn't indicate that I was on active duty, and I got 86 percent of the vote. Even though I'd been gone two years.

After 9/11, the Marine Corps Reserves were looking for people to volunteer. I was IRR, Inactive Regular Reserve. I filled out everything online and I didn't hear anything, didn't hear anything, so I started calling people I know and eventually got orders for Quantico. I demobilized early from there to be able to join this unit and come to Iraq. I didn't know why, but I wanted to come to Iraq, because it's an unfinished chapter in my life. I've been in the Marine Corps Reserves over 30 years and I've never deployed anywhere. I'm not the type of person that hides in the corner. I had to go. I had to be here, be a part of it. Women and men, everyone wants to be involved in this war. It's just something about being a Marine.

I wouldn't trade this experience, this opportunity to be here, working with the Iraqis, for anything. It's nerve-wracking. The convoys, and stuff around you getting blown up, getting shot at. You have to take care of yourself and stay alert.

I meet with Adamson at Camp Fallujah, informally, in the smoking area in the little green patch of ground behind the Public Affairs Office (PAO) between the building and the awesome HESCO barriers topped with sandbags that ring the entire perimeter. HESCO barriers (so-called because of the company that makes them—their name is stamped in large letters on the sides) are three- to five-foot-high collapsible, plastic fiber-impregnated containers that look like, when opened, square cardboard boxes inside vinyl chain-link fencing. They are filled with rubble to stop shrapnel. If the incoming explosive detonates on the other side of the barrier, you are secure from the millions of pieces of mangling metal shards blasted outward. If not, well, that is the nature of an incoming explosive. One is never sure where it will land.

A rocket had landed 50 feet behind the smoking area of the office two months before I arrived. The force of the blast knocked the media officer, Lt Gilbert, out of his chair and blew in the wall on Col Holbert's desk. Fortunately she was out of the office at the time. It dislodged some 30 years of desert dust from the walls and ceiling, blinding the Marines inside. When it was certain the colonel was safe, the Marines gleefully brought the six-foot-long Russian rocket with its jagged, peeled-back warhead into the office to display it on the counter at the PAO entry, with signatures of all safely present and accounted for.

The smoking area has four tenacious, deciduous trees with long dusty brown pods hanging from their branches. When they leaf out, they will be green for awhile, then powdery beige, as with all vegetation throughout Camp Fallujah that is covered with fine desert sand. There is a home-made plywood bench and three heavy-duty nylon collapsible camp chairs. The PX carries them. There are birds flitting in the trees—a heart-warming, cheery presence in this war zone—sparrows, bluebirds, even an occasional kingfisher who flashes iridescent blue feathers as he dives for minnows in a nearby pond.

Camp Fallujah, so named when the Marines took it over in 2004, was built by Saddam as a training camp for MEK (Mujahideen-e-Khalq), fighting units made up of Iranian dissidents, and was frequented by his sons, especially Uday, who added several luxurious touches—a conference center, for instance, and a luxurious garden area with a cement pond. At the pond there is a pair of enormous black and white ducks—unlike any I have ever seen in the United States. When the Marines discover them nesting, they put up a temporary chain-link fence around the entire pond to keep people away. The garden area was irrigated at one time, and the irrigation hoses are visible running through the landscape. The Marines have no time for that nicety now. There are several feral cats to be seen lurking in the dry, dusty grass and shrubs. Only with great imagination can one envision a green oasis in this reordered military space.

When I first arrived in Camp Fallujah, I had no idea what I would find. I came in by Humvee, late at night, and was too tired to be dismayed by the muddy floor in the tent the gunner found for me. This was where he had been told to leave me, but even he was unsure and walked into the mass of dark tents to be certain I ended up in the right one. It was close to 0230 and pitch black. He put my pack on a folding utility table so it would not be on the muddy floor and as he left, I asked him where the heads and showers were located. He pointed out several light-colored trailers about 70 yards away, illuminated by a light on a single pole in their midst.

The tent was a large space with one cot the Marine had set upright near the front for me—all the others were tossed in a heap at the rear. There was the folding table, a fluorescent light attached to the tent pole, and a combination heater/air conditioner run by a generator outside. I got my toothbrush and my red-filtered flashlight and went to the trailers. When I came out of the head, I was disoriented and could not remember the way back. I wandered for so long I was convinced the best thing was simply to curl up on the gravel near one of the trailers and sleep until someone found me. On one more try, I found the right path and followed it to my tent, which was distinguished from the others only by the shaft of light just barely visible at the edge of the tent flap.

I dug my sleeping bag out of my pack, took off my boots, and crawled in, fully clothed, exhausted. Then I remembered the light—six feet away across the muddy, wet floor. I put on my boots and switched it out, finally settling in, and went to sleep immediately, oblivious to all the noise.

Iraq is loud, extremely loud, 24/7. On the bases, there are generators about the size of industrial dumpsters beside every sizable building or tent that run heating and cooling and lights, day and night. Their din is a continuous roar, like a freight train. There are seven-ton trucks rolling past at all hours and the sound of helicopters and often the thunder of C-130s overhead. Sounds of gunfire are always identified, if you ask, as anything but gunfire.

Waking in the morning, I realize there is no activity in the area of tents around me. Just as I am wondering if anyone knows I am in camp, a Marine pushes the tent flap aside and asks if I am Sara Sheldon. She is Master Sergeant Kelly Ramsey, top sergeant to Col Holbert. She had expected me to be dropped off elsewhere and has been looking for me. I shove my computer in its case and before I can pick up my pack, she shoulders it and heads out. She is probably 5 foot 5, dark haired, and extremely attractive. Right off the bat, a woman Marine, I am in the right place.

In the Public Affairs Office I find Col Jenny Holbert. I meet Lt Lyle Gilbert, who will arrange my interviews and escort me throughout the base, and Maj Francis Piccoli, who is not sure he likes the idea of my writing about women Marines, as if there is a distinction. I assure him I am writing about Marines who happen to be women, and then we seem to have an understanding.

I ask Col Holbert how the Marines view carting around inept civilians with them in Humvees during their dangerous security missions.

"Oh, when they hear their passenger is a woman, they're always hoping for some cute 26-year-old reporter," is her reply.

"How many 26-year-olds do they get?" I ask.

"Not enough," she says.

There is no media in Camp Fallujah, and when I was in CPIC, in Baghdad, there had been very few media people there either. It is downtime for the media, after covering the national elections two weeks before. So rather than park me alone in the media tent, some way away, I am invited to plug in my computer in the Public Affairs Office. My requests of my hosts are undemanding—interviews with Marines on base, no embedding with patrols into Fallujah, so everyone can relax a bit. Partly because of my long-standing friendship with Col Holbert and partly because, after the first day, I become "sort of like 'Mom'" according to the colonel, I am included in activities 24/7 with the Marines. It is more than I had expected and everything I had hoped—to be able to hang out with these women informally, to get to know them better than in a 45-minute interview.

What kind of women join the Corps? I wondered. *Are they ambitious? Tomboys? Aggressive?*

First Sergeant Connie Patrice Arline remembers being 18, just out of high school, and planning to go to college when she talked to a Marine recruiter who sold her on the idea of service in the Marines as full of adventure and travel. When her mother worried about her daughter getting through boot camp and had to sign a permission form, her mother told her, "I'll sign for you, but only because I don't think you'll make it." 1stSgt Arline determined then and there to get through boot camp no matter what. "Even if I make it one day past boot camp." But even though Arline found the experience tough, "stressful," as she puts it diplomatically, at graduation she was proud to say, "'I am a Marine.' I haven't been sorry that I made that choice." That was in 1984. With 20 years of service in the Corps, she deployed to Iraq. Along the way she changed her MOS to 3044—Contract Specialist.

> I'm very proud of having had that MOS. I got a lot of breaks, training, things that will take me well beyond this 20 years in the Marine Corps: negotiating, contract pricing, meeting people on a different professional level. It's been a force multiplier.

Corporal Michelle P. Garza, of San Diego, has just finished her four-year recruitment and reenlisted for another four. She is a Disbursing Clerk.

> At first I was looking to the military for school. My mom raised me and my sister and I wanted her to just focus on my sister and I would take care of

myself—earn my own money, be independent. I had spoken to recruiters from the Army, National Guard, and Navy and they didn't get me. Finally I talked to the Marine Corps and they said, "You might be interested in seeing a graduation." It really got me when I went to a Marine graduation [from boot camp] in MCRD [Marine Corps Recruit Depot].

My friends never expected me to do something like this. I was the girliest of them all. But now they tell me they're proud of me. I hate to say it, but I feel if I didn't go into the Marine Corps, I'd be in the same boat as some of them right now—with kids, trying to support their families. Some are trying to go to school, but don't have the money to do it—trying to juggle work and school. I have some friends that are kind of going down the deep end right now. The Marine Corps changed my life.

Captain Jennifer Blake Morris says, "Our generation never felt like we had limitations. I remember watching movies like *Top Gun,* stuff like that, and I wanted to be Tom Cruise. I wanted to be a pilot." Morris was always interested in the military. Her family included veterans of World War II and Vietnam and her father was in the Air Force. And she was a history buff, reading and watching a lot of history programs on TV. She always felt she wanted to go into the military. Her deployment to Iraq marks eight years in the Corps.

She got into Junior ROTC (Reserve Officer Training Corps) in high school and continued with ROTC in college.

> The Marine Corps appealed to me the most just because it was the hardest, the most elite, the toughest to go into, the biggest challenge. If I could make it in that, that's what I wanted. I wanted to prove myself.

After college Morris completed OCS (Officer Candidate School).

> It was tough, but for different reasons than I thought. I mean I knew they were going to yell at you and like that, but it was different, as though they were trying to weed you out.

In OCS, the course is designed around the core values of honor, courage, and commitment, hardly the sorts of intangibles civilians are likely to be tested on. The concept of honor exemplifies the ultimate in ethical and moral behavior, abiding by an uncompromising code of integrity, and respecting human dignity. Officer candidates are expected to embody the qualities of maturity, dedication, trust, and dependability in order to act responsibly, fulfill their obligations, be accountable, and hold others accountable for their actions. By developing mental, moral, and physical strength, officers generate the inner courage to adhere to a higher standard of personal conduct, to lead by example, and to make tough decisions under stress. Commitment leads to the highest order of discipline for individuals and units.

This can be greatly at odds with many young civilian women's lives where the major challenges are finding a job or deciding on a career, with decisions over how fashionable or flashy a wardrobe is acceptable, how to deal with a corporate world that can have barely delineated or conflicting moral standards, and an environment that is highly competitive instead of cooperative. "The physical part I didn't have a problem with," Morris says.

> In college ROTC we had field exercises, hikes, obstacles courses, and no matter how hard I struggled to get finished, I just felt great! I just felt like I was ready for the next challenge. But it seems like at OCS, their whole purpose was to weed you out, find your weaknesses, push your buttons. It was mentally tiring. You were on the go constantly. Some people make it through, some people don't. It was a good experience.

I wondered, *is this the way they make officers and leaders?*
One of the best lessons, Morris says, is learning to have respect for your Marines.

> In 1998, '99, I was fresh out of basic school, in communications, and I was a section leader—basically the size of a platoon. I didn't really know anything, I was supposed to be the officer in charge, but I knew these guys knew their job and I wasn't going to go in and say, "I'm in charge here and we're going to do it my way."

Morris leveled with them, telling them, "'Hey guys, I don't know all the technicalities of this job. Do it right, make us look good, and I'll be right with you.' I learned a lot from them."...Act responsibly, be accountable, hold others accountable.

I wondered, *is there a sense of wanting to serve? An altruistic drive that draws women into the Marines? Patriotism?*
Alexandra Plucinski, 1st Lieutenant, MOS 0402 Logistics Officer, came into the Corps late, after a university degree, a year at Oxford, and traveling widely abroad, a job with a major public relations firm in New York, and two years at a national nonprofit organization. She was active in coaching kids' swim teams and got into kickboxing. She was restless, wanted to keep her life interesting, and had applied at the CIA, the FBI, the UN, and the Peace Corps.

> Then September 11 happened. It almost made the decision for me. Someone had mentioned the military and I was looking at the Army. But I thought, *what am I going to do in the military? I don't take orders well from other people. I'm stubborn. I'm old.* I did not have a good perception of the military at all. But 9/11 just kind of sealed the idea for me—witnessing it firsthand. You see devastation all around you and you see the response and you see how people rallied together. Every New Yorker was angry and furious. I thought, *you've got to do something.*
>
> I had just come back from Vienna, Austria, where I became World Kickboxing Champion. I was preparing for another fight, and, ironically, had been called to take the State Department Foreign Service exam in a building close to the World Trade Center, but of course everything was shut down.

You get so many options, and I'm not sure where to put my energy. I'd just won the kickboxing championship, but it's just a sport. I thought, *I can fight. I want to do my part to fight this war.* A year later I was at OCS.

My conception of a Marine was a very large man who killed things on a regular basis. They've got a great campaign, a great advertising strategy. When Marines are out in public, they definitely look like Marines. They've branded this whole image of themselves that they've held for centuries. It's a boys club, elitist. I thought, *How am I going to make it? Can I deal with it? Can I deal with the BS? Are they going to accept me as a woman?* I wasn't intimidated, but I really did not know what I was getting myself into. I thought it was going to be really stressful, but I wanted to be the top, the best.

I was in great shape, and in kickboxing you learn to channel and focus your energy and aggression. You know how to protect yourself. I was scared of getting injured. I'd had injuries before and that was something I didn't want. I thought, *if I hate it, it's three years out of my life.*

Then I went to Basic School—every Marine goes to basic school for six months. It was a lot of hard work. There are certain officers you admire and who motivate you, others you learn to hate. You don't understand that sometimes. You have to be a good follower before you can be a good leader. You have to understand what you're asking of your Marines. You should never give a Marine a task you're not willing to do yourself. And that's how I became a Marine.

Marines who wish to become commissioned officers must comply with basic qualifications to be admitted to OSC—a combined score of 1,000 in the verbal and math sections of the SAT, or a combined score of 45 in verbal and math in the ACT, or a composite score of 120 in General Science, Arithmetic Reasoning, Mathematics Knowledge, and Electronics Information on the Marine Corps Armed Services Vocational Aptitude Battery test. They must also be a U.S. citizen, have at least a bachelor's degree at the time of commissioning, be between 18 and 28 years of age, meet normal medical admission standards, be eligible for security clearance, and possess high moral character.

OCS consists of ten weeks of training—a screening and evaluation program—followed by The Basic School (TBS). Marines emerge from OCS as second lieutenants. In TBS, also affectionately referred to by some Marines as "The Big Suck," newly commissioned officers spend six months in courses on leadership and techniques of military instruction in marksmanship, map reading, communications, infantry tactics, weapons, organization and staff functions, drill, command, military law, logistics, personnel administration, and Marines history. Nearing completion of TBS, officers select their MOS.

These training programs are unique to the Marine Corps and are experiences that result in lifelong friendships as bonds are forged regardless of differing MOS, gender, and civilian background.

September 11 was also a strong influence on Lance Corporal Crystal Groves, when she was only 15. "After that, I kind of knew that I'd do something. I was thinking about the military, but I wasn't sure which branch."

When she decided to join the Marines,

> My mother had to sign the papers because I was only 17, and she didn't want me to go. But by then, I had posters all over my room and talked about it all the time. I talked about it at supper, and I think she felt I really wanted to do it.
>
> I loved boot camp. It's very much a challenge. The Marine Corps teaches you a lot about yourself, what you didn't know you could be. It makes you quite confident about a lot of things. I remember when I first received the title "United States Marine," I'd look down at my uniform and see that tape that says "US Marines" and it feels good to see that on me. Just to know that I went through all that and made it as far as I have. It's been a lumpy road, a lot of discipline, learning how to deal with that.

LCpl Groves drives seven-ton trucks, and she laughs, "They're not as big after you've been driving them awhile. I also have a license to drive Humvees, but there isn't as much demand for that."

The guys like to drive the Humvees—they think it is cool. Groves picks up and delivers supplies, sometimes "outside the wire," meaning outside the base. Detainees, suspected insurgents, are also live cargo in her trucks at times, in the city of Fallujah.

I ask these women if they really knew how tough Marine Corps training was when they signed up.

Corporal Brandie Collette, MOS 5811, Field Military Police, is an artist —painter, sculptor, photographer, and more. Not her first career choice, the Marine Corps was something she wanted to do to start off her life and to make her father proud. "He worked very hard when I was younger. He didn't get to spend much time with me. I wanted him to be able to look back and say, 'Hey, look what my daughter's doing!'"

As for it being a personal challenge, she says,

> I like to accept work that seems impossible for a woman to do—for anybody to do—and do it. The Marines were the hardest, and there were very few females in the Corps. It was the best thing I could think of.

In her early 20s, Cpl Collette has six siblings who are all proud of her, especially her brother, now discharged from the Army Reserves, and her father, who is proudest of all. Military Police (MP) work was not an interest of Collette's—she had asked for Public Affairs or Combat Photography. But she finds some satisfaction in MP work. "You get your job done, and it's always nice to know you've done the job well. I do the job I'm told to do."

Col Jenny Holbert began her career as an enlisted Marine and remembers becoming a Marine after recruit training at Parris Island, South Carolina, where all women Marines are trained. "You're just so full of piss and vinegar—so full of yourself. But it takes a lot longer to be a Marine in your head—to get it, to really be there."

The wall above Captain Amy Alger's desk in a plywood reinforced building that serves as her billet and her office holds several photos of her with various Washington Beltway celebrities—President Bill Clinton, Colin Powell (then Chairman of the Joint Chiefs of Staff), First Lady Hillary Clinton, and Senator John Glenn (former astronaut), among others. Capt Alger is a Communications Processor, and she began her career in the Corps as an enlisted Marine. After Photography School in Washington, D.C., Alger was assigned to General Mundy, then Commandant of the Marine Corps, as staff photographer. This was a glamorous life for a young, enlisted Marine—three years traveling the world, photographing on Capitol Hill and at the White House—quite a contrast to her Spartan office now, at Camp Taqqadum, a large air base west of Fallujah. Surrounded with gravel and sand, her small shack has three rooms: a bedroom, her office, an anteroom that serves as a meeting room, and outside, a small porch with a cooler that holds bottled water and MREs (Meals Ready-to-Eat). Showers and toilets, for Alger as for everybody else, are about 75 yards away. But Alger has one of the few private quarters on base, by choice, to be closer to her unit. She converted a building uninhabitable by humans into serviceable living space, but deprived herself of the relative comforts of officers' quarters.

> I joined the Marine Corps just after Christmas in 1989 and went to boot camp at Parris Island in April. I was a college graduate when I went to Parris Island. I went to college on a full scholarship to play basketball. It was just one of those things where I wasn't really focused on academics at that point in my life.

When she graduated, playing professionally overseas did not really appeal to her as much as trying to get started in a career. But she did not want to go right back to school, so she chose to join the Marines.

> The Corps was very parallel to where my life was at the time. I was very comfortable with a regimented life-style—get up in the morning, go and work out, eat breakfast, go to classes, come back and have some time to do some studying, go to practice. Groundhog Day everyday. The Marine life-style was something I thought would be a challenge and would make me feel like I was part of a well-respected organization.

It was quite an honor to have General Mundy promote her to sergeant and then, when she was selected for Officer Candidate School, pin on her second lieutenant bars when she graduated.

Marines refer frequently to Groundhog Day as a way to describe the "same old" repetitiveness of their life in Iraq. It refers to the movie of that name, made in 1993, starring Bill Murray, that depicts Murray waking every day destined to repeat the day before over and over with every detail exactly the same.

Capt Alger wears two hats at Camp Taqqadum: as executive officer of Headquarters and Services Battalion and as company commander of Communications Company. As for being a Marine, Alger says,

> I have flourished in this gun club. I love it. It's who I am. I mean, my identity is so tied to this now it's almost scary. I'm a different person outside of my work, as you can guess by my hobbies [she rides a Harley], and being a Marine makes things interesting in your personal life. It cost me a marriage. I made my decision and it was a career decision. I never looked back. People don't understand female Marines. It's very difficult. Most people cannot comprehend, or grasp, or maybe they just don't want to or are scared by it or put off by it. I love to go out, put on a nice cocktail dress, go out on the town, and I do, but the truth is I'm a Marine. And people don't really know how to deal with that. And that's okay.

I think many people wonder if women can really make good Marines, being the weaker sex. I talk about that with the Marines I interview.

Staff Sergeant Alison Arnold is a Radio Chief in Iraq who joined the Corps in 1994 after high school in Shepherd, a little town in northeast Texas. She remembers the support the whole town showed the troops when the Gulf War started.

> Our town came together and we had this big celebration when the units came home. I felt like, *that's something I want to do. I want to serve my country.* And being from such a small town, I wanted to get out and see a little bit more of the world, and travel. My senior year I started thinking about going into the Marines. All the recruiters from the various branches came to the high school. I remember seeing the Marine recruiter in a fancy uniform that looked like something I'd like to wear. I talked to the Army, the Air Force, and the Navy, but the Marines won me over, so I signed on.

SSgt Arnold overheard some of the boys in her high school saying, "I'm going to join the Army because the Marine Corps is too hard."

Arnold's response? "That just made me want to do it—'Okay, I'm going to show you guys.'" As for being a woman in the Corps? "I don't think— you know, honestly, I don't think people can fully understand, unless they walk in our shoes, the kinds of things we have to deal with." Arnold is a single mother with a 9-year-old son back home. She is also a Radio Chief, in charge of 22 Marines who operate single-channel radios, a short-range communications system.

"I was ready to come out here," Arnold says.

When everything kicked off in 2003, I was stuck on the drill field. I say "stuck" because most of us, that's how we felt. We were excited. We wanted to be out here. We wanted to come over here and be with our fellow Marines. Okay, finally we get to do what we joined the Marine Corps to do. I love the Marine Corps.

As for actually being in Iraq, she says,

You know what? I don't get too stressed out here because I'm more worried about my Marines. If your Marines see that you're affected by it, then of course it's going to affect them. When you're lying in your rack by yourself, you might think how close the incoming round was that day, but the longer you're out here, the less it bothers you. It's only when you start thinking about going home and you get incoming. If it gets pretty close it makes you think *hey, I don't need this! I'm getting ready to go home!*

I interview First Sergeant Laura L. Brown, MOS 9999, in her modest office at Camp Taqqadum in a busy building with little privacy and a lot going on. As a first sergeant, she manages Marines with several skills in Iraq: food service, PX, postal service, mortuary affairs, disbursing, and legal services. She began her career in the Marine Corps after graduation from high school in San Antonio.

I'm Hispanic-American. When I was ready to graduate in 1984 I didn't know what I wanted to do. My parents divorced when I was 5. In my community, it was "find somebody to marry and have children," and that's not what I wanted to do.

Brown learned about the Marines when a classmate told her about visiting a recruiter. Brown went on her own to the recruiter and decided that was her way out. The recruiter tutored her in math to prepare her for the military entry exam. She scored so high in math on the test that she spent the next 17 years in disbursing. "I knew when I joined the Marine Corps that I would be here 20 years. This is where I found myself."

After making the rank of sergeant, Brown spent three years on the drill field, training women recruits to be Marines. She picked up gunnery sergeant quickly after that and was deployed to Iraq in 2004 with an MP company providing rear-area security. What is rear-area security? When convoys of trucks carrying supplies for the bases travel the treacherous roads through Iraq, there is Humvee escort I had ridden in. As Brown puts it, "They're vehicles with big machine-gun mounted weapons. It's impressive and it's scary at the same time." Yup, I had the same feeling.

Since they were moving through combat areas, 1stSgt Brown carried a M9 service pistol, even though by law she is not allowed to be in combat. As a first sergeant she was leading the Marines and was responsible for keeping the troops going—making sure they were fed, their feet were dry, their health was good, and they were properly trained.

When she accompanied her Marines outside the wire, there were occasions when they did not return to base and billeted in the field. She shared the billet (sleeping space) with the male Marines—there was one other woman in her unit, a lance corporal—in tents with rows of cots. In situations like that, many women Marines told me they changed clothes inside their sleeping bags, and took turns sharing sparse makeshift shower facilities and latrines.

The U.S. military bases in Iraq are enormous, and there are sometimes two and three chow halls and Internet cafes on each base because there is no transportation within the base and often it is too far to walk to chow from a billet or an office. On base, women enlisted Marines have their own large tents as do the men; officers billet in smaller, sometimes hardened (plywood-reinforced) spaces or adapted Iraqi buildings. All share gender-segregated shower and toilet trailers, hauled in to the bases and cleaned and supplied with water by contractors. There is usually a line or cluster of white metal trailers with doors marked "Women's Head" (toilet) or "Men's Shower." For every eight trailers designated for male use, there is one for women, reflecting the number of Marines of each gender serving in Iraq. Off base, outside the wire, there are no such "luxurious" facilities, so everything is shared.

1stSgt Brown told me,

> You know, you're always amazed. When we were in the rear, preparing for the field, we trained all the time, but all the training in the world can never prepare you emotionally and mentally for what you're going to endure out here. Looking at the young faces, you're just amazed. In the rear, you're yelling at them about trivial things, about bouncing a check, about paying child support, about getting up on time and getting to the company and not forgetting their gear. But they get out here and they man these turrets, man these machine guns, and they bark these orders, these 20-year-old people. It just amazes you, and swells your chest with pride. Really.

She is the information conduit to her commander and as such provides advice and counsel regarding her Marines.

All the Marines in Iraq with differing MOS skills work interdependently, providing the support and morale for the combat troops. Civilian employees of the Department of Defense (DoD) sometimes volunteer to go into Iraq to work in PXs and other jobs, as Brown says, "and put themselves in harm's way. They earn a lot more money than we do, but they come out here to a combat zone and put themselves in harm's way."

Indeed, one of the DoD American civilian volunteers I met at the military airport in Kuwait told me she volunteered because the pastor of her church told her the war was Jesus's punishment for all the babies that had been killed in the United States (by abortion) and it was her duty to go and atone for that sin. Everybody has their reasons for going to a combat zone. Most civilians go because it is financially worth it. Some are richly paid, earning as much as $200,000 a year, tax-free, working as KBR contractors.

Workers, called Third-Country Nationals (TCNs), come from nearly every nation in the world and do everything from driving trucks to food service, laundry, and reconstruction. Some are very poorly paid, compared to Western standards, but still come to work in a stressful war zone when they cannot find work in their own country—some for as little as $20 for a 12-hour day. If they take a day off, it is without pay. There has been criticism in India and other South Asian countries of their countrymen being subjected to "human rights abuses" and working in "U.S. Slave Camps." Still, workers sign up to work abroad, often not being told the work is in Iraq.

They have no medical coverage, and no armor, though the bases where they work are often under attack. Hundreds of thousands of Iraqis are unemployed, but the United States discourages hiring them for fear of insurgent infiltration of the bases. KBR reports that 40,000 TCNs work in support of the U.S. military in Iraq.

Many KBR skilled employees are U.S. military who have served in Iraq, know the dangers, and return for short periods to earn high salaries using the skills they acquired in the service—particularly many private security guards. The Marines interact with these higher-paid civilians every day and seem to avoid being disgruntled about the disparity in pay. It has to do with their code of honor and their focus on the mission. There are not enough U.S. military personnel to keep the forces in the field without outside help.

The Marines, Brown tells me, serve as security at the chow halls, but all the food service is done by contractors who are foreign nationals. The Marines also make sure food is handled, cooked, and stored correctly and that foreigners working with it observe the requisite USDA food safety rules that are far more stringent than those in most other countries.

After Brown's years as a disburser, she picked up first sergeant.

> That means you leave what you've known for 17 years and become a manager of people. My counterpart in this MOS is a master sergeant in the Marine Corps. A master sergeant is doing the same thing he's been doing for 17 years, but he brings the technical proficiency. I bring the managerial skills.

Whatever their job, they are all equally at risk in the combat zone.

Often I ask the Marines I interview if they view the Marine Corps as a career with on-the-job training. Is it a way to get money for college? Is this why women join?

First Lieutenant Blanca Binstock joined the Corps at 17.

There was not much for me at home, you know. I have two older sisters and an older brother. I kind of wanted to get out of the house. Typical story: get out of the house, no college money—I wasn't focused. I thought I'd join the Marine Corps, get some money for college, do some college while I was in, get out, finish college, get a career, get married.

She laughs,

I did it all backward. I joined the Marine Corps and then got married. I met my husband at MOS school at Camp Johnson, near Camp Lejeune, in North Carolina. We had the same MOS, we were both PFCs, and we were both 18. I don't think many people thought it would last, but when you find the right one, you find the right one. It'll be our tenth anniversary in May.

When we were still enlisted, we put in packages for a commissioning program. We both got selected, went to college together, and got commissioned the same day. Then we went to Basic School together. Now I'm 28, and I've been looking forward to deploying here. I felt like it was my time. It's time for me to give these guys a break, do my part, get some experience. This is the real world, this is what we train for. There's no better learning environment than actually being here, training in this environment.

If I hadn't joined the Corps, my life would have been so different. My life would have been terrible. I watch these Marines who are so young, so very young, and have such integrity, such dedication out here. I ask them to do things and none of them ever say, "No, I'm not gonna do that," or "Nobody told me I had to do that." I can't imagine a bunch of kids their age at home doing that without an argument.

I interview Lance Corporal Mary Kathryn Heathcoat, MOS 0621, Field Radio Operator on her birthday. She has a twin sister also in the Marine Corps.

At first, I was going to join the Army, because that was the first recruiter I talked to, and when he saw my entrance exam scores he said, "We definitely want you." But my mom said no. The next year my sister told my mom that she wanted to join the Marine Corps, and mom said, "Okay—if your sister goes." I was okay with that, because I wanted to join the military anyway, and it didn't really matter. I guess I was glad when I joined the Marine Corps because people have a different respect for the Marines, and also they have a different respect for female Marines because it's so hard.

My sister wanted to be the first female sniper, but her rifle scores weren't good enough. [The Marines Corps has not allowed women to be snipers because it is a combat position.] We ended up going to comm [communications] school, but I was a week behind her because I was a "broken" Marine. That's when we got separated. I graduated from Basic Warrior Training in boot camp with a fractured femur. I didn't say anything when it happened because I didn't want to stop. I wanted to keep on going. But it just got worse and worse and worse. I graduated on time, but then I had to go on leave [to heal] and come back. I think that was a good experience, because when you go back to Parris Island you're a Marine, no longer a recruit, and the time I spent there I had respect from the CO and the staff, and I got to see a different side. It was better than the guys who just went from basic training straight to MCT [Marine Combat Training] school. I was more confident going to MCT.

Heathcoat left Camp Taqqadum for home several days later, as her sister, in the States, prepared to deploy to Iraq.

Corporal Terianne Anderson is 20, has three years in the Corps, and is in Aviation Maintenance Administration.

I think the reason I came in before I was old enough was that my father was a Marine. He was in Vietnam. Being a Marine seems almost to be in your genes. He raised us with a love of the Marine Corps. We celebrated the November 10th birthday of the Corps every year since I can remember. When I got to junior high school, I hadn't really decided what I wanted to do. I wanted to go to college, but I wanted to do something else with my life before I went to school. My brother joined the Marine Corps about then, but my father never pressured us to join. My brother's three years older. He'd had a year in college, but wanted to join the Corps before he finished. It sort of opened the door for me.

What had been an accepted part of life for Anderson then became exciting.

I was really hard core. I was really excited about going. I couldn't get enough of learning about the Marine Corps. Boot camp was challenging, but I loved it. Every aspect of it. I like to do things that challenge me. I'd go back and do it again if I could.

Cpl Anderson is involved in the vital job of aircraft maintenance as a logbook clerk.

Every aircraft has a logbook. Every engine has a logbook. We log everything —flight time, maintenance, when an engine's pulled, repaired. Right now we're in charge of maintenance for 18 Cobras and 9 Hueys. We send messages about the aircraft as well. If an aircraft has to go in for repairs, we notify the Wing, or higher up.

Anderson is married to a Marine Reservist who is working on getting his commission. He was in Iraq before they were married, and Anderson was angry because she was not deploying, too. "I really wanted to be here. Everyone was going, but they told me I wasn't going anywhere." She wrote several letters requesting deployment, but got nowhere. When her husband returned, they decided to marry and she asked again about her chances on being sent to Iraq. They told her, "No, you're going to be stationed in the rear till you get out. Just live with that."

"I thought, *all right, I'll establish a life,*" Anderson says,

and two months later, I went in to work one day and they said "go pack your bags." On a personal level, I'm glad, because if I hadn't come out here I'd always have the feeling I hadn't played my cards. My husband wants to be in the Marine Corps for years. His father's also a Marine.

Now Anderson finds it difficult because her husband has to be the one at home while she's at war. Still too young to legally drink, Anderson is very much in harm's way.

Sergeant Major Suzanne Renee How holds the highest rank for an enlisted Marine. She is a 23-year veteran of the Corps. Women sergeants major are rare.

I went to the University of Nebraska–Omaha for a year, where I was born and raised. I had some unreasonably high expectations for my college experience, and when they weren't met, I decided that I'd try something really different. When you think about the Marine Corps, it's sort of like the song "New York, New York." I figured if I could make it through boot camp, I could do anything after that—it would be easy. I just wanted to go through recruit training. I had no idea what was going to happen after that. I fell in love with the Marine Corps. That's the only thing I can say. That's what happened.

I felt that how [Marines] aspire to really high standards, how we treat each other, even how we treat our enemies, was something I could throw my life into. I wasn't chasing the almighty dollar. [Marine] values were the same as my personal values. And the physical challenge, the mental challenge—I had a wonderful time.

That attitude aside, SgtMaj How did not stand out in boot camp.

I was terrible. I was! Physically, no problem, but I didn't blossom until I got out of that restricted environment, as soon as I could start making some decisions for myself. I got put in charge right away. I enjoy that—the freedom to make decisions within a given framework. I seem to excel at that. I saw that as a creative outlet for me. I didn't feel it was restrictive. I felt it gave me a lot of freedom.

She laughs. "I just decided right then and there I wanted to be in charge."

How served her first 13 years overseas. She started in Scotland, then went to Okinawa, Korea, the Philippines, Hawaii, and the Panama Canal.

Then I volunteered to be a drill instructor. I trained officer candidates. I spent two years at Quantico in Marine Corps intelligence. Then a posting came up at the Naval Academy for a female gunnery sergeant, so I went to the Academy for two years. You are paired up with an officer and you teach a company of midshipmen, who have selected the Marine option, Naval Science 404. That teaches them about Marine Corps tactics and procedures. You get out there and teach them to climb a rope—all that stuff.

The Academy is kind of a strange place, but it grows on you. It's a unique environment. The traditions are so important to them. The midshipmen are real young and they're real smart. They're either real gullible or real headstrong. There are a lot of contrasts at the Academy.

When you meet other Marines, they teach you things about loyalty, dedication, and devotion to duty. Many I've met are very inspirational to me. I see how they handle a situation and the impact it has on me: I'm going to carry that around with me and use it to help other Marines in the future. Like dropping a pebble in the pond, the ripples keep going out and out and out. Marines continue to affect Marines who affect Marines who affect Marines. I never dreamed I could be part of an organization where that could be true. Because it's not true on the outside. I know it's not true. But it's true in here. Now, even the guys who see me walking around wearing sergeant major, and I can see in their eyes, they're thinking "I can do that." And I think *damn right you can!* I tell my Marines, "the only thing between you and me is, I've got 22 years of strength and you don't. If you want to be sergeant major or master guns, or a commissioned officer, all you've got to do is dream big and don't let anyone tell you no. Believe in yourself and you can do it. Don't let anybody tell you no. I'm living proof of that."

In Camp Fallujah I interview a young Marine who had become an unwitting poster person for the Marines—Lance Corporal Jessica Kane. Kane is 0621, a Field Radio Operator. She has been in the Marine Corps for a little over two years.

I was 21 when I joined. I had just gotten suspended from college, and I had to come up with something to do for a year. My father was in the Marines and taught me about the pride the Marines have, so I thought about joining the Marine Corps Reserves, putting in a year, go back to school, do the one-weekend-a-month thing and grow up a little, maybe mature some, and not be so wild and crazy and not get in trouble anymore. I definitely didn't plan on being out here, but it turns out to be a good thing.

I was in a reserve unit in Washington, D.C., and we were activated. I grew up some more out here. I'm on a six-year contract, so I have a little over three years left. I'll have had a lot of experience when I get out. I want to finish school.

I joined because of my father, but I knew it was the best thing I could do. Dad was honest about it not being a piece of cake, and that it was difficult for men and women, and sometimes tougher for a woman to rise above stereotypes. But I joined because it is the best, and you don't become the best without sacrifice and hard work.

Before I was deployed out here, I could tell people were impressed because I'm a Marine. I see the looks on their faces. Sometimes they're shocked. I mean, they think, do they even *let* females in the Corps? Sometimes people tell me they'd be terrified to be a Marine and they ask me what it's like. They know what's expected of a Marine and they look up to me. I tell them it's great. It's tough, all right, and you have to want to be a Marine to get through it. Maybe it's my personality or the great Marines I've had a chance to work with, but I've never had a problem with being a female Marine. The guys in my shop, in Civil Affairs, treat me like a little sister, and sometimes they're overprotective. It's the same when we're in Fallujah. They're always looking out for me.

Kane was selected to be the driver for her commanding officer, so she drives into the city of Fallujah and provides security for him while he is in the vehicle and security for him when he wades into the crowds of Fallujans to talk, ask questions, and hear complaints. She's proud of the fact that she is "outside the wire" doing something constructive.

> I don't know if it's being out here in Iraq, but being a Marine definitely puts your life in perspective. When you're young you do so many stupid things. At home the biggest worry would be running out of beer before midnight. Looking back, that's stupid. That's not even close to what's important now. Here, you realize what you value most, and there are more important things in life.

After Kane wrote home to her father about her surprise and overwhelming respect for Lieutenant General John F. Sattler, the commanding general, when he personally showed up at the chow hall and served Thanksgiving and Christmas dinners to the Marines in thanks for all they were doing, her father sent the letter by e-mail to friends, and it became a widely circulated fan letter about the Marines. She wrote about General George William Casey, Jr. coming to commend the unit for their work in Iraq and that all the guard posts that day were manned by officers instead of PFCs and lance corporals. The command had decided that the Marines would have Thanksgiving evening off and have time to enjoy their dinner.

To see this, Kane says, "filled me with pride. I am so honored to be a part of an organization like this. Marines taking care of Marines with such unselfishness." As a result of her letter to her father, there were articles written about her and she was commended by her senior officer. She began receiving packages from children and organizations all over the States—she was on her 175th such package the day I interviewed her, three months after her letter became widely known—full of candy, jerky, games, comics, cookies, toiletries, socks, Bibles, gum, soap, drawings, letters, all of which she shares freely with the Marines on base and the people of Fallujah. Well, perhaps she does not share the Bibles.

Lieutenant Colonel Cindy Atkins is a grandmother, a 23-year veteran of the Corps, and is in her first deployment to Iraq. What was going through her mind when she enlisted for two years in 1975?

> I was a senior in high school. I knew everything. My parents knew nothing. I had to get out of the house. I wanted to go to school. I wanted money. A Marine recruiter came to my school and a couple of buddies, male, joined and went through boot camp. They came back and talked about the G.I. Bill. If I'd just come in for two years, I'd qualify for the G.I. Bill. In two years I could get out and go to college. I'd have a job. I'd get away. I was sold. I'd lived there my whole life. The idea of seeing the world, doing something, getting out of Missouri—they sold me. I came home and told my parents what I wanted to do. At that time, women, even if they were 18, you still

had to have your parents' permission to join. The males didn't. My mother said, "No way. Your uncle was a Marine in Korea. He had a woman in every port." My father—well, he did it for four years in World War II, so what the heck, why not? Six months later, I graduated and was off to boot camp. Later, my mother came around and realized it was the greatest thing I'd ever done.

When I first came in, in 1975, women were only about 2 percent of the Marine Corps—very small. Everything was segregated. At Parris Island, I had a male instructor who taught us drill.

After graduation from boot camp, Atkins was stationed at Parris Island and served under two chains of command: one, male, for the office in which she worked with other male Marines, and then an administrative chain of command of women officers in charge of all female Marines.

There were different rules across the board. For one thing, if you got married and wanted to claim him as your dependent, for medical benefits, you had to prove you fully supported him. [Men were never asked to verify sole support of their wives.] I've seen a lot of changes. We had our own separate uniform of blue pants and little collared buttoned-up blue shirts and sweaters. Then I got married and I was pregnant. I wasn't sure I could meet Marine Corps standards, and be a mother at the same time. So I got out. I had the G.I. Bill, so I went to school and had my other son. At the time, I felt my marriage was coming apart and I missed the Marine Corps, the camaraderie. It was a place where, if I worked hard, I got rewarded for it. I had done well. In 18 months I had made it all the way to corporal. I missed it, and I knew it was a sure thing—that I could succeed at it. So I went back and asked if I could come back. They let me back in. Then I applied for Officer Candidate School and was accepted. I went through that with my two kids—my youngest two and a half. I don't recommend that to people. Everything is a full-time job. Being a Marine is a full-time job.

My kids are very independent. They cook, they clean, they do toilets. We ran a regimented schedule. They were up on time. I'd fix them a hot breakfast and while they were eating, I'd be in the shower and getting dressed. I'd come down, they'd go up—wash their faces, brush their teeth, comb their hair, grab their book bags. Out the door they'd go—school, preschool, day care. And they did sports. They did all the sports. They played soccer, basketball, baseball, football. They just figured out how to juggle everything. They'd clean the house on Thursday nights. It was all laid out and it worked. Our weekends we had free to play, because there wasn't any housework on weekends. As they got older, it was part of their allowance. They worked out what chores they had to do on Thursday to get their allowance on Friday.

Thursday, the Marines explain to me, is the traditional day for cleaning the barracks for Friday inspection. If the barracks do not pass inspection on Friday, you do not get leave for the weekend.

Atkins completed her time in the Marines and retired. She went to work in the private sector. Then, in 2003, she got a call.

I thought it was a joke. I had come home from work one night and there was a message on my answering machine, from a friend, a Marine. "Hey, would you be interested in coming back? We think we have a job for you." I laughed. I retired. I did my 20-some years and retired. I never heard of them bringing someone back from retirement. My friend told me, "No, we can bring you back." So I agreed—anything I can do to help. But I told them. "I'll come back as long as I can be deployed. I don't want to come back and sit at Camp Pendleton. I trained for 20 years and never did anything real, so if I come back, I want to deploy." I don't want my grandkids to have to come over here. I'll take care of it and let them stay quiet back in the States.

Atkins had been employed by Pfizer Pharmaceutical for the previous two years. The company has given her military leave and is holding her job for her return. She feels that Pfizer is very like the Marine Corps with rules and regulations and core values very similar to the Corps. Her job in Iraq is rather like human resources in a civilian company.

The main thing is personnel accountability. We have to know where everybody is all the time. Especially with all the kidnapping threats and the intimidation that goes on. And then casualty reports. Any time a Marine or sailor is injured or killed, heaven forbid, we have to process it, get personal information on it: name, rank, serial number, MOS, hometown, the unit they're from and the circumstances surrounding what happened. That is all put together and sent electronically to Quantico, back in Virginia. Then they will notify the unit based closest to the next of kin to notify the family. During the battle in Fallujah we had 83 killed and over 800 injured. If the wounded were medivaced back to us, we'd send them to Bravo Surgical for medical treatment. They saved a lot of lives. We tracked the men here being treated and those in the field constantly, making sure everybody in their unit was accounted for.

A lot of Marines are getting maimed, losing limbs. We haven't been through anything like this since World War II. Vietnam was bad, but I've never seen anything like this. But it's different. I tell you, there are so many organizations that have popped up, nonprofits, from everywhere, that are supporting us out here. The American public has been great. I heard about when Vietnam was over, when people came home from there, how ugly it was. But here we get so many care packages and letters, it's so supportive. It's very heartwarming. I put the children's letters and drawings up in my office. One of them is a little handprint.

When I rotate out, I'll retire again and go back to my job. This experience goes back to when I first joined. If you're going to join, why not join the best. I have no regrets. It's been hard, it hasn't always been easy, but I have no regrets.

Col Jenny Holbert, of Public Affairs, told me of making visits to the wounded at Bravo Surgical and working them through their anger at being out of the fight. The Marines are extremely emotional and in denial about being unable to go back to join their buddies. With four men to a fire team, they are well aware that the team is extremely vulnerable when one man is wounded and taken out. The fire team trains together for months. They know all the hand signals and keep each other alive because they interact so well together. So the wounded Marines are enraged—really pissed off—that they are not able to go back, and they argue with the doctors—even in cases of amputation. Visitors to the Marines ask if they have notified their family. Almost always, the Marines do not want their families to know. It has to be emphasized that their families need to hear from them instead of hearing it from a buddy. Satellite phones are always available to wounded Marines for calls home.

Holbert talked about visiting and talking with a tall lance corporal leaning against a wall, concerned about a much shorter noncommissioned officer (NCO) who was lying on a stretcher in the recovery room after surgery. Neither would be returning to the battle, but the lance corporal told over and over the story of how the NCO had saved him—and everybody in his unit. He was hyperanimated from shock and pain-killers.

"In truth," Holbert says, "there's no way either of them are going back [into battle] and a possibility neither of them will make it [out of Bravo Surgical]."

In case of the death of a Marine, a casualty officer is assigned to notify the next of kin. It can be anybody—often someone who comes from the area where the Marine came from. Sometimes a close friend in combat with the deceased Marine will request to be assigned as casualty officer. The Marine Corps tries to make accommodations for a personal request and, in special circumstances, has been known to fly a combat Marine out of Iraq to accompany the body home.

I had no idea what stories I would hear from these women Marines when I undertook the journey to Iraq. Perhaps, I considered, what some of my liberal friends tell me is true. Perhaps these Marines have all been brainwashed. Boot camp, some critics suggest, reduces recruits to blithering idiots—"maggots" is a term used by drill sergeants—and then fills their grasping personas with fancy notions about the unique attributes of the Marine Corps, encouraging them to become killers—baby killers, some say—with dedication and impunity.

Instead, the Marines I meet in Iraq are extraordinarily courageous, thoughtful, articulate women who do indeed spout the creed—honor, courage, commitment—but who have gone through their rigorous training voluntarily and are proud of their dedication to the Corps, their contributions to their country, and their loyalty to their commander in chief who may, in assessing the best interests of the country, put them in harm's way.

3

THE GUYS' GUN CLUB

LtCol Loretta Reynolds commands a communications battalion of 1,200 men. Her rank pretty much precludes having to deal with Marines who may question her ability or her professionalism. But there were times, as she was coming up in rank, when she says she dealt up front with incidents of gender discrimination.

I meet with Reynolds at her office in a craggy landscape of peaks made of camouflage nets that constitutes the Communications Command, just across the road from the second ring of the walled compound that is Camp Fallujah. The camp is huge and is arranged in three rings—the fortified outer wall, a large area of tent billets and service areas and then a second ring of wall, and finally, a small third walled area that is command central. There are trees and what used to be formal gardens in some of the inner areas. The buildings are old Iraqi barracks, office buildings, and motor pools, with some elegant halls and lounges sprinkled throughout.

Everywhere you look the setting is a natural tan—the road, the tents, the camouflage, vehicles, uniforms, boots, even the sky when the breeze carries fine sand. It is impossible to guess how large the communications battalion is. Your eye is fooled by the netting. Lori Reynolds is distinguished by her height and the ease with which she wears her responsibility. She has a husky voice and the engaging smile of a woman who is clearly centered and in sync with her surroundings. She wears her M9 service pistol on her thigh. When she points off in the distance, to the city of Fallujah, just a few miles away, or at the high satellite towers rising above the landscape that are her handiwork, she emanates authority and seems comfortable in her command.

As for having any difficulty being a woman in the guys' gun club, she says,

> I think we're past that. I hope we're past that. But, it's funny, my sergeant major, a man with 23 years in, showed up at my command last January, and he'd never served with a woman before. He came up through the grunts.

Now, he's taken over his first command as sergeant major, and here's this woman. He told me, "I just want you to know, I'm going to give this a chance. My wife told me to give it a chance." He was up front about it.

So I said, "Well that's great, Sergeant Major, because neither one of us has a choice. You don't have a choice, nor do I. So that's good advice your wife gave you to give it a shot." We laugh about it now, because he's phenomenal. He's awesome. Every once in a while you run into those types of things, but he's about the only guy that could get away with it in this command. I didn't take offense at what he said. He'd never served with a woman.

I think if they sense you're a professional, there's no issue. You'll have your 5 percent who are idiots, and I'm pleased to let them know that they're idiots. Since I was a lieutenant, I think, I've felt as long as they think they're being led well, they don't care. That's my experience.

And I feel that it's always true that women Marines are harder on other Marine women than the men will be. We take care of our own to make sure we're doing the right thing, setting the right example. Because all they need is one bad example and we're all affected by that.

Marines have a reputation for respect—honor—which is part of their code. Traveling through Iraq alone, I walk and talk with many Marines, all of whom, I reflect, are inadvertently looking out for me.

Climbing down off a Black Hawk, a three-foot jump, in the middle of the night at BIAP, a Marine behind me taps me on the shoulder and points to my pack, which I am struggling to keep off the ground on my wrist, my other hand being occupied with my computer case. The engine noise of the rotors is so loud that I cannot understand what he is saying. Finally, he just takes hold of the pack, motions with a circle of his finger that I should turn around, and then helps me get it onto my shoulders. I shrug it in place and follow him out onto the dark, rocky flight line. Walking out of the downblast of the rotor blades, I am nearly blown off my feet. The pack is easily 35 pounds and top-heavy. The Marine turns and grabs my arm, steadies me, and then mouths "Okay?" before pushing me ahead of him and falling in behind.

I spend a lot of time, mostly in the dark, waiting for flights. Leaving Camp Fallujah to travel to Camp Taqqadum, about a 20-minute trip, on a CH-46 Marine helicopter one night, I am escorted to the landing zone by Lt Gilbert, of Public Affairs. It is 1930 and already dark. I am manifested in, giving my last name, first name, unit, social security number, and blood type to the manifest officer standing in the dark, using a small flashlight, marking on a clipboard.

The officer points out the line I am to stand in and Gilbert shakes my hand, wishes me well, and then gallantly asks two young Marines standing ahead of me in line to look out for me. The lines for departing flights are delineated by ropes tied to stakes, perpendicular to the landing zone. There are three or four. The line next to us has about 30 Marines waiting.

Gilbert had gotten some intel that the inbound helo from Al Asad (my flight) was delayed two hours, but we elected to go out to the flight line in case that intel changed and the flight was on time.

In front of us is a road, about 50 feet wide, then a slight rise up to the landing zone (LZ), a long runway with no lighting. It is a clear night, two days away from a full moon. Everywhere you look there is bleached white moonlit sand and gravel—not a tree in sight. All the dark shapes of waiting Marines and gear and weapons look as if they have been dusted with a fine white powder. The sky is bright with stars, and we can see many constellations. In the distance is the glow of lights from Camp Fallujah. Suddenly, there is a massive eruption of orange flames with showers of red sparks. In the night, all eyes are drawn toward it, but then, everyone turns away and resumes the wait.

A rickety bus arrives periodically at the end of the waiting zone, near the terminal (a shack that has a sign saying "PASSENGERS NOT ALLOWED"), and Marines, huge with battle gear and body armor, who have been squashed in the insubstantial seats, heave themselves out and lug their gear to the manifest officer to be checked in.

CH-46s arrive in threes, this evening, about every 30 to 45 minutes. Other times they fly in pairs, or alone. The pattern is varied frequently. They drop out of the sky and materialize in front of you on the LZ. You can hear them coming, and follow the sound as they circle around to come in, but they are just shadows until they land. They fly without lights, only IR (infrared) beams that the pilots see with their night vision goggles. They line up on the LZ, touch down with engines running, and the crew chiefs run back to assist the exodus off the lowered ramps in the back. Marines in battle gear erupt out the back, down the ramp, and trot out to muster in front of us. The manifest officer, with a yellow light marking his vest, directs them toward the terminal to be checked in. The sound of the 46s is loud, even through our earplugs. The whap-whap-whap of the rotor blades creates tremors we can feel through our combat boots. They are awesome.

The manifest officer calls out the group of Marines next to us, and they shoulder their gear and run out into the maw in the rear of the 46. The bird digests the Marines, the ramp goes up, the bird hovers in place a moment and then lifts straight up, and lurches forward to fly out into the night sky. We turn our backs, hunch over, squeeze our eyes shut, and cover our faces to avoid the powerful blast of burning wind and sand created by the rotors as they ascend.

All night the helicopters come and go, the sound of the rotors a continuous assault on the ears. But it is a welcome assault. The sound means someone is coming for you—it is a connection to someplace else—home base, a new assignment, or R&R, or maybe just a way out.

It is cold, about 30°F, and the two Marines in line with me are soon digging through their mountain of gear to get sweaters, Gore-Tex, and gloves. I have on silk long johns, an underarmor shirt, a long-sleeved tee, a fleece jacket zipped with the collar up, and my waterproof windbreaker with the hood up over my helmet and tied under my chin.

At first, the two pace the ground and talk to themselves, using the usual "fuck" this and "fuck" that. After I consider that I might be out on this flight line a long time with them, I decide to strike up a conversation.

They are MPs, coming in from Africa, to replace two MPs in I-MEF (1st Marine Expeditionary Force) who were wounded and medivaced out of Iraq. They are 20 and 22 years old and have already served in Afghanistan. They seem so young, like school athletes waiting for the team bus.

Talking with me, all the F words disappear, and it is "Ma'am" this and "Ma'am" that. They suggest I go sit in the waiting room—the usual huge tent, with cots, chairs, and buckets for cigarette butts. It is a dark hulk next to the terminal, with heavy canvas over the door to keep the light in. You have to take all your gear with you if you elect to wait in the tent, out of the cold, and you lose your place in line. They assure me they will watch my pack and save my place. But the tent is just a smoke-filled space, so I choose to stay with them.

After two and a half hours, at 2200 one of them runs off to ask about our flight and, sure enough, it has been delayed at least two hours. That is standard operating procedure. Flights can be canceled if a bird gets sick or there is a heavy wind- or sandstorm, which is often. All flights are unannounced until they arrive and are not certain until they take off or are en route. We kick the sand, try to stay warm, and talk. We perch on the gear, but it is cold, not moving about. They tell me they have arranged for a truck to transport their 14 bags of gear out to the helo when it arrives, and they will throw my bag on top. We tell each other our life stories. I am amazed at how much of the world these Marines have seen and fought in during their young lives. They are amazed that I would put up with the inconvenience of Iraq to come out here to get the Marines' stories. My inconvenience, I tell them, is exponentially unequal to theirs.

Finally, at 2315, three 46s touch down and the manifest officer comes running to motion us forward. We walk/run out to the ramp—I am carrying my computer case, and they have their weapons—we all have our helmets on, earplugs in. We run up the broad ramp in the rear of the aircraft, find a seat along the side, and buckle in. The 46s are enormous compared to the small space in a Black Hawk. There is a wide, empty aisle between the rows of Marines facing each other along the sides of the helo. The gear is piled in a mound in the back, the ramp is raised, and we lift off. It is exhilarating—after four hours of waiting for a 20-minute flight to our destination. We fly at 200 feet and, looking down as we approach Camp

Taqqadum, it is difficult to see the enormity of the air base. It is an endless expanse of moonlit, dusty white roads, buildings, and tents. When we disembark, one of my Marine buddies grabs my pack, throws it on the truck with their gear, turns me to face the huge aerodrome about a football field away from us, motions for me to follow his friend, and falls in behind.

At Camp Taqqadum, Lance Corporal Crystal Groves, whose MOS is Motor Transportation Operator, drives seven-ton trucks along those dusty roads and outside the wire, as well. She enlisted when she was 17. She is blond, quick to smile, and says she has not had any real problems with male Marines.

> You need to work like you're a Marine. Male, female, it doesn't matter. The guys seem to like it if you'll get out there and just do the work. They see that and they think *she's one of us.*
>
> It's tough at times, but we all train the same way, whether they say we did or we didn't. If the guys say things that are wrong, you have to tell them, let them know you don't like it. Some guys will go along with that, others won't. But if you keep telling them, keep doing it, keep doing it, pretty soon they just quit.

GySgt Amanda Vargas is an Administrative Chief at Camp Taqqadum who has done her share of training and leading Marines. She has been a drill instructor and martial arts instructor and feels that Marine women have come a long way, but still have a way to go to be completely accepted as full partners in a war zone.

> Some of the men still have the mentality that women shouldn't be out here in Iraq. At times, no matter that we've accomplished as much as they have, or better, they still won't acknowledge who we are. And in the past I've met my share of male Marines who have never worked with female Marines. I usually lay down the law when I first meet my Marines and so, early on, they didn't like me too much. It took them a while to see my abilities.
>
> Also, I'm a fast runner. Early on, when we were in training, on a run, there was a lot of competition, and a lot of the men didn't like it. I heard them saying, "Don't let that you-know-what beat you." But some of the Marines wouldn't stand for that. They'd say to the guys, "You know what? She's a Marine. She's our sister. You just don't do that." I think a lot of the guys just put you down so they'll feel better about themselves.
>
> Another buddy, who's a grunt, an infantry guy, went through drill instructor school with me. He's gotten a Bronze Star from Afghanistan. A heck of a guy. But back when we were in school, he'd never worked with female Marines. We had a fitness test, a three-mile run. There were only two men out of 45 Marines. They were first and second and then there was me. My buddy says he heard footsteps behind him and turned and saw me and said, "When I saw you were a girl, I thought *no girl's going to beat me!*" So he killed himself to beat me. We laugh about it now. After that we were in the martial

arts course together and on the pistol range. He saw how I could fight and told me. "You're a tough little shrimp. You're pretty tough." And when he saw me shooting he said, "Here we go again. I've got to compete with your ass again." He beat me, but he said, "I can't let you beat me. You're everywhere I go!" We make a joke out of it now and he teases me. "You're such a girl. You'll never beat me because you're a girl." But he also told me, "You're right up there with the best of us." It's really nice to hear that. Of course, there are some who'll never get it. They'll just find a reason why you're not as good as they are.

Vargas is strikingly attractive with black hair smoothed diagonally across her forehead. She has a husband back in the rear, who is also a Marine gunnery sergeant, and a young son whose tenth birthday, two days away, she will miss.

1stLt Alexandra Plucinski, who hails from Chicago, is a Logistics Officer and now, in Iraq, a combat commander in charge of a platoon of Marines who take convoys into Fallujah and the surrounding area. She has an open, trusting gaze that gives no hint of her varied experiences in life.

I do what every other Marine officer would do to take care of their Marines. If my Marines have problems taking orders from a woman, they keep it to themselves—they respect me enough not to say it.

They're great. They're a great bunch. They're so young, with no experience in the real world. They're just kids. But they're professional. We didn't stand up together [as a unit] until we got into the country. We didn't have time to do a lot of proper training. But seeing where we are now compared to where they were when we first got here—it's amazing.

A lot of these Marines were just out of high school. Fresh faces, afraid, terrified of dying and leaving their families behind. Then to watch them put all their tactics, techniques, and procedures we taught them together—you know they can do the job. A lot of them are just 18 or 19 and they've got kids already, and wives. I talk to them all the time about their lives. You just want to give them the best life they can have. I do a lot of counseling.

When the platoon came together over here, you have to be able to rely on the Marines to your left and right and count on their training. You think they're not paying attention, but they all do their job in the end. Sometimes they call me "mom" instead of ma'am. I guess because I'm older. But I look out for them and they look out for me.

Capt Jennifer Blake Morris is a Communications Officer with eight years in the Corps. She says that she hears inappropriate jokes at times, but overall she is treated very professionally.

It seems to me, when you're going through OCS and Basic School, if you give a hundred percent, act professional, and know what you're talking about, that's all they care about. They probably test you more than they would your male counterpart. When I had my first platoon, I had a big gunny, a war vet from Desert Storm, Somalia, and Panama, and my master guns was another big guy. They didn't even like officers, let alone here's some female lieutenant coming in. They definitely tested me. They always asked me questions they knew I couldn't answer and tried to make me stumble.

Morris chose to take the offensive and give as good as she got.

I wondered why they were being such jerks and started dishing it right back to them. "I don't know, Master Guns, isn't that your job to help mold a young officer? Why don't you tell me what the answer is?" Eventually, we became tight. I still talk to him to this day. He's a good friend. He's retired now. It seems they just test you to see if you can handle the pressure, if your skin is thick enough. They're not going to tiptoe around you. They're going to treat you like a Marine. If you play the female card and say, "Oh, you hurt my feelings," or, God forbid, you cry, oh, my God, forget about it. If you want to be in the boys' club, act like a Marine.

LCpl Mary Heathcoat is a Field Radio Operator at Camp Taqqadum who, to her total surprise, found herself being counseled for fraternization with the Marines in her group. She was the only female in her team and felt singled out because of that.

All of us go to chow together because these are the guys I work with, and we're all just friends. But one day the chief told me he needed to talk to me, and I went with him into a room with all three of the officers. I was surprised. They went through the counseling sheet with me. And they were all males. That isn't the way it should be done, with no women officers.

On base, everybody hangs out together, I mean, going to chow and all, because if anything happens, we'd all be together. Somebody thought another Marine in the group and I had something going on. It was very, very, very, very petty. I mean, other people are doing worse things than going to chow together. We never held hands or anything—sometimes we didn't even sit together. It just made me mad. You know, we've got people here doing things they're not supposed to, but nobody says anything to them. But one little thing that shouldn't even have been brought to anyone's attention and it made me look bad. And it got out that I was counseled. One day when I was working, one of the male nurses asked me to do something and I said, "Don't worry about it, sir, I'm on top of things," and he said, "Oh, I heard you are!" I thought, *where did that come from? Why would he say something like that?* I don't know why.

One day when I left work I felt the chief was following me and so I went to the XO (executive officer), but he told me a suspicion wasn't enough. But I think he may have talked to some of them because a couple of weeks ago it finally just kind of settled down. You know, for a while I felt like I was getting looks like I was a bad person. I didn't like that. They made me feel like I was dirty or something. Now, no matter what time of day or night, I have to call a female buddy from another unit and arrange to go to chow with her, or walk back and forth from work with her. I can't hang with the guys at all.

I asked Heathcoat if she planned to file a complaint or do anything further about it. Her answer was a shrug. "We have a job to do. I have to move on."

LtCol Cindy Atkins wears her dark hair pulled severely away from her face and looks like a stern but loving mother as well as a professional Marine. She is both. Called out of retirement in her 40s to return to administration and deployment to Iraq, she remembers some discrimination against her gender in her early years. But she was motivated, she says.

> I had a goal, in my years in the Corps, and I kind of reached that. So when I was called to come back from retirement, I thought I might get promoted again, and the only opportunity would be to be active in the Marine Corps again. What I was called in to do, I'd done before. I just knew there was a certain point I wouldn't go above. That's the old boys' gun club. What you need to do is figure out how to fit in, be successful, be the best you can. You're not always going to be good enough. It is an old boys' gun club. But when you're doing your best, and doing your job well, it doesn't matter.

At 23, LCpl Jessica Kane has two years in the Corps and thinks being in the Guys' Gun Club has been pretty positive. She is sunny and upbeat and perhaps a little amazed to find herself a minor celebrity in Iraq when her e-mail home about being served Thanksgiving dinner by her general was sent all around the nation.

> Sometimes, when I'm driving in the city, or back in the rear, the States, I'll get a look like "I can't believe that—it's a girl, and she's a Marine?" but I like that. When I'm driving in Fallujah, I'll see Marines do a double take that I'm out there, too. Once I heard a Marine talking to a couple of soldiers who asked about me, and he asked if any female soldiers were coming into the city. They said, "No, in the Army the females aren't driving into the city." The Marine was bragging about how female Marines are all over the area.

Cpl Brandie Collette, a Field MP in Iraq and a photographer and artist in civilian life, thinks it is very interesting being a female in the Corps.

> Sometimes we get along great and other times you can definitely tell that they feel intimidated that there's a female doing their job. I just picked up rank, and there are a lot of guys that haven't picked up for a long time, so there's jealousy. But sometimes they treat me just like a little sister. They're very protective. It really all depends on the day.

1stSgt Laura L. Brown, with 22 years in the Corps, is on her second deployment to Iraq, now with the Service Company. She's dealt with male Marines throughout her career, and in her first stint in Iraq, in a combat situation. She has an aura of confidence about her, and a slow, warm smile. Listening to her story, I hear the discipline and the professional attitude that has brought her to the top of her field as a Marine.

It is a guys' gun club. But you learn how to get around it. I've always told my male counterparts that women have to work twice as hard. But if you know what you bring to the table, it just becomes who you are. Instead of it becoming a challenge, you just find another door to go through. Eventually they realize—when you're re-assigned, they will shake your hand. They will tell you, "I had a misconception about you," and that's good.

I think because we're so different—you know the saying "men are from Mars, women are from Venus"? Truly, they can't help themselves. I don't think they mean anything by it, it's just the way they are. You're going to have your womanizers, you're going to have your bullies, you're going to have those who treat you like a lady. I really believe, and I tell this to every female who comes in the Marine Corps, it's the product you portray. It's the example you set. If you come in and expect and demand courtesy and professionalism, you're going to get it.

Another first sergeant, Connie Arline, with 21 years in, also has come to terms with her passage through years of working with her male counterparts.

It's been very tough, but I think you just have to make up your mind that you want to do a thing and you don't let anybody take that away from you. There have been lots of situations in classes and squads I've been in where I've been the only female. When I compete in that situation, I do it pretty much with all the female Marines in mind, just to show them we can do it. But it's been tough.

I think you have to realize it's a man's world. You might have to deal with comments you don't want to hear. They will make remarks, but I'm strong. Over the years I've gotten to the point where I ignore it, ignore it, ignore it, show them I can do it. Now [as first sergeant], I'm in a position to say, "Hey, we're not having that." We go through the same rites of passage that they do.

After ten years in the Corps, SSgt Alison Arnold has stronger feelings about being a female Marine.

I was a drill instructor from 2000 to 2003 and I tried to teach these young females that without them doing anything they would have certain preset images portrayed of them. Regardless of who you are, how well you do, you'll be one of several things in people's eyes if you're in the Marine Corps. You'll be the one that's sleeping around if you have a male friend. You'll be the standoffish one if you don't talk to everybody. You'll be put in a category. So I tell my recruits, don't give them any reason to validate any of those concepts. Most of them think they know it all. I was that way when I was a recruit. They think, "Yeah, yeah, yeah." But when they begin to experience it for themselves, you hope they remember what you were trying to teach them.

1stLt Blanca Binstock started out as an enlisted Marine and then went through OCS. She has experienced being a female on both sides. She thinks that men just were not really educated about women's place in the Marine Corps and that women make good Marines.

> When I was a sergeant in Okinawa, I worked with a lot of infantry, sergeants, who had never even talked to a female Marine. Because they were around infantrymen all the time, they had misconceptions about what we did in the Corps. Some were afraid to speak to you for fear of getting in trouble for saying the wrong thing.
>
> The Marine Corps mandates that we have classes on sexual harassment and equal opportunity, but I guess they just never thought they'd have to actually interact with us in the field. After I spent some time with them, I made some good friends among the infantry officers. So now I don't get much negative feedback. Most of what I get is curiosity. "What do you do in this situation? What does your husband think about you doing that?" But nothing like, "You don't belong here." I've never gotten that.

Flight training for female Marines has been available only for a dozen years. Twenty-six-year-old Tara Russell is a first lieutenant flying Huey helicopters in combat support out of Camp Taqqadum. Her father was a Marine pilot as well. She meets me at a cluster of adobe and plywood buildings at the edge of the flight line and finds a briefing room where we can talk. It is cool and dark in the room, in contrast to the bright sun making black, cutout silhouettes of the helicopters visible outside the window. 1stLt Russell exudes tremendous self-assurance and is clearly at ease in her surroundings.

After flight school each Marine lists his or her preference: helicopters, jets, or C-130s. The Marine Corps looks at its needs and assigns their personnel accordingly. As Russell explains it,

> You learn to fly Hueys in a training environment. The training is in series: hundred level, two-hundred level, three-hundred level. You do the basic familiarization, instruments, that kind of stuff when you're at the hundred level. You're in a more protected environment. Then they kick you down to a fleet squadron. That's where you get more tactical stuff.

Does Russell ever get told, "You can't do that"?
"No," she says.

> I've got two supportive, strong parents who told me, "Whatever you want, go do it. You can do it." But I find people are surprised at what I do. Sometimes in the commissary when I'm shopping, I'll be in my flight suit, and older Marines, retired Marines will say to me, "They don't make Marines like they used to anymore. They didn't have female pilots like you when I was a Marine." It surprises them. Actually, last night at chow, I was sitting down and there were two young sergeants. One of them looked at me and said, "Are you a mechanic?" "No, I'm a pilot." It doesn't dawn on some of them that there are women doing that, and that I'm this young, doing that.

Russell eschews makeup, although some of her mechanics wear it. When she takes her long hair down, she takes some guff from the guys. "You're such a girl," they'll say to her.

> I tell them, "That's just the way I am. You're not going to change it. I'm not going to start swearing like a sailor. That's not who I am. I'm a lady, and I'm a Marine, and that's the way I'm going to conduct myself." Some of them don't like it, and say things to me. But I have a good friend, a captain, who told some of them, "Look, you don't know what it's like to walk in her shoes. She has to put up with so much crap from you guys and she does it. She doesn't say anything. She just feels it. So until you've had to deal with it, don't begrudge her for having long hair or whatever else you have a problem with. If you don't like it, that's your problem. That's not her problem. She's a woman. She's going to show her femininity. If you don't like it, oh well."
>
> I've found that if they can get away with talking about you in a negative way, then you're okay. So if they call you names, question your sexual preference, question your ability at work, or your reputation, you're okay. They have to have something to talk about. They put me down for femininity. It bothers me that they can't accept me for who I am—someone who did the exact same thing they did, a girl who got through flight school. I don't have to prove anything. I'm just doing my job right now.

During this interview, Capt Amy Malugani, the Public Affairs Officer for Camp Taqqadum (TQ), who coordinated and escorted me to my interviews and who is days away from rotating back to the States, gets a call on her cell phone telling her that the flight that she had been notified earlier would take me to BIAP that afternoon was canceled. Later, leaving the chow hall after lunch, she gets another call telling her I am rescheduled on another CH-46 and to get me out to the flight line immediately.

In an all-out scramble, we rush into my tent and scoop up everything— sleeping bag, jacket, travel kit—and cram it into my backpack. I pull on my flak jacket and grab my helmet. Malugani runs ahead to borrow a pickup from administration to drive me out to the airfield, and we speed over the rocky dirt road to the huge hangers that mark the old British airfield. The British built these huge Quonset-hut-shaped hangers in 1919 when they were helping build the new country of Iraq. There is some irony here. The hangers are enormous, perhaps 40 feet high, of concrete, and windowless. It is dark and cool inside, despite the huge yawning open end. The two runways, 12,000 and 13,000 feet long, were undamaged during the U.S. invasion for the most part, so Taqqadum is a major supply base and military airfield with a Marine aircraft wing servicing everyone from Fallujah west to the border with Saudi Arabia.

Flights arrive on the huge open ground space containing the runways with regularity; some are sticks for pax—the Marine jargon for passengers (pax) on any given flight (stick). It is a long, rocky trek out to the flight line.

Inside the big cement hanger that serves as a terminal, dozens of Marines are sacked out on the cement floor, oblivious to everything except the barking of their surname that will summon them to a waiting flight. There are perhaps two dozen folding chairs, most sprung so that sitting is impossible without balancing backward. In the large, dark room there is a 36-inch TV showing current American DVDs, endlessly. It is an open cocoon-like space with the high cement dome overhead, giving a false sense of security.

When I arrived here, six days previously, I had hardly noticed any of this, because it had been so late. That night, I remember seeing Capt Malugani step forward to meet me as I stumbled off the field, and once again, I was grateful for the competence of the Marine Corps. Again, my fears of arriving at an air base in Iraq without knowing where to go, or what to do, were abated. On that night of my arrival, Malugani had waited hours for my flight, rather than make the long drive back to her hooch, only to be called back when I finally arrived. That night, driving me into my allotted space in a Marine tent, she had babbled all the way. Worn down, dead tired, and only about six days from rotating out to the States, it was 0200 and she had been up for 20 hours. Her replacement had already arrived, and she was talking about her life after Iraq. She rambled about the dangers, the excitement, the boredom. She was sad to leave, eager to go, and very proud she had the opportunity to do her part.

Now, back at the aerodrome on my way out, I look and am struck by how much the space is unlike a commercial airport in the States—no amenities, no restrooms, no place to sit; portapotties out back and a big metal cooler with MREs and bottled water for the taking. Check-in at a small desk is minimal—last name, a glance at my press credential around my neck, a notation of my blood type (always that chilling detail), and "We'll call you." Everyone is dressed the same except for me, but no one bothers to turn and look at me.

Capt Malugani is dark-haired and pretty, with big, dark eyes, and a girlish smile. She chats easily about the women Marines at TQ and their backgrounds. As liaison for the media, she knows her way around the large air base. She was with the media who embedded with Marines during the Battle for Fallujah in 2004, so she has definitely been in harm's way, although her MOS of Public Affairs is strictly a supportive role. She tells me she once fought a weight problem (hard to believe) and that women Marines in Iraq are fighting all sorts of feminine health problems with no recourse to the simple medical treatments available in the rear. The medical units are geared for men and treating casualties, not handling simple hygienic problems for women. Many women, she tells me, stop menstruating when they arrive in Iraq due to the high level of stress. While this may be a worry personally, it is a blessing in many ways when heads are often trenches or a patch in the desert and carrying sanitary napkins or tampons is just one more thing to find a pocket for and some kind of disposal. Early on, there was a problem getting sanitary supplies, and the call went out to the rear to send the tampons they could not get in the PXs. Friends and family in the United States responded in spades, and in every shower or toilet trailer wherever I travel, there are boxes of every brand and type of sanitary napkin available to anyone. This does not solve the problem of carrying them when they go on a convoy or travel outside the wire, but it makes things very much easier on base.

On this afternoon that I am to depart, Malugani and I sit and talk for a short time; she tells me that she had a male Marine officer who mentored her and told her the worst situation to be in, as a Marine, was to be a beautiful female who does her job well and is smart,

> because the older male Marines can't stand it that you can still be a girl, still be a good Marine and your Marines follow you. It's frustrating. I can show up in makeup and still be a leader, still put my foot down; I'm confident and my Marines love me. The older guys just don't get it.
>
> Often I've walked into a situation, a new assignment, and had to follow in the footsteps of a female Marine who had her own problems. I didn't want to be labeled as bad as or as good as the woman I replaced. So I just decided, "You know what? That's not me. I don't have to prove myself. I'm just going to settle in and be myself." And within two or three months, people would recognize me for who I am. You just have to do that. Because if you don't you'll just be fitted into a category. And we don't need to be fitted into categories.
>
> For instance, the Gunny came in the other day and said he needed to use the printer. He told me he never used the printer and didn't know how. "This is your opportunity to prove yourself to me," he told me. I told him, "Gunny, I don't have to prove anything to you. You have to go down to the help desk and get them to help you like everyone else."

Eventually, it becomes obvious that I might have a long wait for a flight, and Malugani and I agree she needs to get back to the base. It is getting dark. I move to a chair up near the open end of the aerodrome where there were two people waiting: one a Marine officer, another a civilian who appears to be an Iraqi woman, perhaps a translator. Indeed, that is who she is. Her name is Anna, and the Marine is escorting her to her next assignment. She has a big, clumsy, hard-sided red suitcase with her. Anna had fled from Iraq just after the First Gulf War in 1991, getting to Yemen and then working for a year to get sufficient funds to emigrate to Canada. The difficulties of her situation, as an Iraqi woman alone, without a man to front for her, were enormous. But in Canada she had a pleasant life and made a home for herself until the United States invaded Iraq in 2003, whereupon she volunteered to return as an interpreter for the U.S.

forces. This kind of sacrifice and bravery fits in perfectly for working with the Marines.

When I ask for her opinion of the Iraqis regarding the recent elections, she says the Sunni women (the majority of the population in the Marines' area of Al Anbar province is Sunni) do not understand the importance of voting because they do not trust the talk about their "rights." They never had them, do not know what they are, and have never had anyone "give" them anything unless it was trouble.

> They realize that whatever they have, as has been the situation in their entire lives, and during the time they lived with their parents, can be taken away from them at a moment's notice. So what's all this talk about "rights"? It's not even something they can eat.
>
> The Iraqis, especially, the women, have no idea who to vote for. They go to vote if they are assured it is safe to do so. And your Marines provided that security. Their main concern is if they can find food for the next day, and water. And if their house will still be standing by morning. They are fearful when their children leave the house. They have the Marines coming to search their homes in the middle of the night for insurgents, and they relive the fears of the days when Saddam dragged their men away for unknown reasons. It is devastating for them. Most Iraqis look to their imams or sheiks for instructions as to how to vote.

Anna thinks it will take a generation for the Iraqis to feel the change is permanent. She does not believe a democracy can be formed in Iraq because there is so much tribalism. Given the instability of the region for thousands of years, there is only loyalty to their immediate tribe. A sense of nationalism can come only after they see a benevolent Iraqi government working on their behalf for enough years to make them believe in the possibility of another way of life, another kind of civilization.

As Anna says, "They've been in survival mode for so many years that they do not even think beyond the next day or the few people they interact with and can trust."

She refers to the grand exit strategy for Iraq and the forming of a functioning Iraqi government—terms discussed *ad infinitum* in the American media and among governmental figures as meaningless debate among the uninformed.

Anna, who follows the news while she is in Iraq, thinks that very few in the States have a clue as to what the real situation is over here. She feels the journalists write the macho, sensational stories—the bombings, insurgent attacks, beheadings, and torture—whatever is immediate. The Department of Defense and military VIPs who comment on the situation on the news shows either have not been here or were here two hours one time and take the reports from the officers who briefed them and add their spin as "observers."

In the late dusk of the day, one of the many flights of helicopters that have arrived and departed Taqqadum finally has a seat with my name on it. I load my pack on my back, don my Kevlar helmet, stuff plugs in my ears, and trudge out over the darkening rocky field, following the line of Marines to the back of one of the big CH-46 helicopters idling loudly on the LZ. Inevitably, a Marine comes up behind, and mouthing something like "I'll take that, ma'am" but inaudible with the roar of the rotors, lifts the pack off my shoulders and indicates I am to follow in his footsteps.

4

CULTURE CLASH—WOMEN WARRIORS IN IRAQ

One thing that is noticeably absent from most areas I travel to or through in Iraq is Iraqi people. Beginning with the landing at the military area of BIAP, and ranging through a hundred-mile radius, the only Iraqis I see are in Baghdad and inside the IZ where I go to pick up my press credentials.

The Coalition Press Information Center (CPIC) is located in the Baghdad Convention Center, also the Coalition headquarters in Baghdad. The Army maintains offices for the press on the second floor and a media center with Western-style electrical outlets and free Internet connections (for members of the press). There is still damage in the building from the American bombings, but the gaping hole in the wall in the press center is covered by a tarpaulin, and it is business as usual. The building is used by the Coalition and now by the interim Iraqi government for many functions, including visits from VIPs from the United States. It is where the Iraqi parliament now meets and was the site of a suicide bomb attack in early spring 2007.

While I am at CPIC, waiting for a return flight to BIAP to meet a Marine convoy that will take me to Camp Fallujah, I go into the media center and am able to send my first e-mail back to the States. I am welcomed by the middle-aged American lady (a contractor) who oversees the center and its complement of sometimes frantic journalists, and I share microwave popcorn with the few network and newspaper representatives present.

The IZ (International Zone, or Green Zone, in Baghdad) is heavily fortified, surrounded by "T walls" of blast-proof and reinforced concrete slabs called barriers, coils of razor wire, chain-link fences, earthen berms, and armed checkpoints. There are three types of barriers, commonly referred to as Jersey barriers (2 to 3 feet high), Texas barriers (6 to 8 feet high), and Alaska barriers (12 to 16 feet high) All three are used at places in the IZ. The zone is defended by Abrams M1A1 battle tanks, armored vehicles, and .50-caliber machine guns atop Humvees. The IZ is almost totally self-sufficient, and personnel can walk freely, jog, shop, and seek medical attention in secure clinics and hospitals.

The helicopters land at a secure LZ, and passengers are bused to a collection point where there is a loggia and picnic tables; everyone waits while the luggage is all arranged in neat rows to be sniffed by K9 dogs for explosives. We maintain strict silence and do not move to allow the dogs to work without distractions. Across the street is the imposing bombed-out hulk of marble that was the Baathist Party headquarters. The building is several stories high and has an elegant, relatively unmarked marble façade masking the black hole visible inside—the results of a smart bomb that reamed out the interior. An Army corporal, on guard at the collection point, offers me a chunk of the marble to take home as a souvenir. Roughly the size of a bar of soap, it is sand-colored with specks of grey and black. It could be the detritus of any patio or marble stairway anywhere in the world, but I take it as a treasured memento. Armored SUVs drive into the adjacent parking area and pick up contractors, officers, government officials; eventually a van comes for me to take me to CPIC.

Driving through Baghdad, I see landmarks that I remember from watching the beginning of the war, on TV at home. It is an eerie feeling when I realize I also remember names of hotels that were bombed, and famous intersections where suicide bombers detonated cars—and I am there.

At the Convention Center I am searched by an Iraqi woman in a chador, with only her face visible. She wears white gloves and pats me down in a perfunctory manner. When I turn, after going through security to pick up my backpack and computer case, I notice her gesturing at me with a quizzical expression on her face and talking to another woman beside her. *Perhaps not too many gray-haired women in armor and fatigues come through the door,* I think.

After an hour at CPIC during which I am photographed and IDd and informed that Lt Gilbert and Col Holbert, of Public Affairs for the Marine Corps in Camp Fallujah, are keeping in touch and inquiring about my progress (most reassuring), the Army captain in charge graciously escorts me to lunch, along with some of his staff, at the Al-Rasheed Hotel, which is home to many U.S. military officers and occupation officials. Lunch is free to all credentialed Americans and military personnel. The hotel corridors are lined with souvenir shops crammed with every manner of bric-a-brac, their proprietors standing in front of the glass storefronts, quietly beaming, hands folded in front of them, knowing Americans do not appreciate being hustled.

Inside the ballroom, now an enormous cafeteria-style chow hall, contractors, private security guards, and military personnel eat at large round banquet tables. Only here will I see weapons laid on the richly patterned carpeting of the floor beside the chairs. Everywhere else, soldiers and Marines wear their M16s during meals. I share a table with a loquacious hulk with a Scandanavian accent from a security firm who informs all who care to listen about the inadequacy of the well-known Blackwater security firm, his competitor. I am oblivious. It is my first meal in 36 hours. Lunch is an all-you-can-eat buffet with every manner of American food you could desire. Field green salads, hamburgers, yogurt, pasta, tuna salad, salmon, chocolate pudding, roast beef, baked potatoes, fries, cheese cake, hot dogs, cottage cheese, fried chicken or barbecue, chocolate cake, ice cream—it is all there.

Later that night, as I am about to bed down on a sofa in the Conference Center outside the CPIC offices, a call comes through that the Marines have found a seat for me on a flight that will take me back to BIAP to connect with a Marine convoy heading to Fallujah. I am one of a handful of passengers on the short, 15-minute flight aboard two Black Hawks from the secure heliport in the IZ in Baghdad, at 2300 hours. It is dark and we are flying low. Part of Baghdad is lit, and I can see the blue lights atop the minarets attached to the mosques. I see darkened houses below, patios with plastic chairs, cars parked in gravelly yards, and sometimes laundry swirling in the helicopter downblast. Ten minutes into the flight, the two Black Hawks sit down in a field, engines running, lights blacked out. The crew chief, gesturing and forming his words with exaggeration, in order to be understood over the deafening noise of the rotors, points for all of us passengers to disembark and follow a crew member out of the chopper to stand about 75 feet out in the dark, rough stubble of the field. We scramble over the cables, leaving our packs behind, and jump off the three-foot doorway, trotting away from the chopper and stand, mute, as it is impossible to talk over the noise of the engine, wondering what danger has caused the flight to temporarily abort. After about five minutes, the crew chief gestures at us to come back, and we run back to scramble up, climb over wires and packs to strap ourselves into the open cabin. We lift up and complete the remainder of the flight into BIAP. There is no explanation given for these setdowns—you assume that they are for reasons of security.

Once I leave the IZ, I am never again aware of seeing any Iraqis. Other than a dozen chow hall servers or Internet café attendants (who could be Pakistanis, Indians, Samoans, Somalis, as well as Iraqis), there is no human evidence that I am in a foreign country. I am surrounded with personnel in the ubiquitous camouflage uniform. The military branch, rank, and name tags on the cammies change, but without the concrete bunkers,

HESCO barriers everywhere you look, sandbags, and concertina wire, I could be on a military base anywhere—even Southern California.

Some of the military personnel stationed in Iraq have the same experience. They fly in on military transport, travel by military convoys or helicopters, and live, completely surrounded by security, on U.S. military bases in country.

The Marines I interview, and some private contractors I chat with, admit to some concern that Iraqis employed on the bases constitute a possible danger—not in themselves, as they are screened for security and searched on entering or leaving the bases, but because they are liable to coercion from insurgents, once they leave the base, who threaten their families unless they divulge information such as location of command centers, numbers of troops, motor pools, et cetera, to provide targets for mortars lobbed into the base. More recently, Iraqis are simply murdered just for being suspected of working for the American military.

Capt Amy Alger, executive officer of H&S (Headquarters and Service) Battalion and company commander of Communications in Camp Taqqadum, tells me about the heated activity in mortar and rocket attacks prior to the Battle of Fallujah in November 2004.

> We have [Iraqi] nationals that work here on base. They have eyes, and sites, that they had obviously marked before we came. They have base models that they formed out of knowledge of their prior position here. So they're a little more clever than a lot of folks would like to give them credit for.
>
> How can we weed out the insurgents from locals that work here? We don't know. We can't be sure.

For women Marines who travel outside the wire, in combat or on supply or administrative missions, it is an eye-opening experience. SSgt Gianniana Pinedo, an MP, helped with the first elections, in January 2005, in the city of Fallujah. She is small, strong and trim, with her hair pulled back tightly, and obviously able to take care of herself.

> You've got to be careful with the Iraqi men, because once you give them any leeway, like smiling, or looking at them when they're trying to get your attention, they all flock around you. So I have to make it clear it is not permissible, put my hand up, and warn them away. Once they see the reaction I have to them, they back off and give me a little respect.

Capt Jodie Sweezey, of Civil Affairs, also interacted with Iraqi men in Fallujah at a new health center over a period of several months.

> I noticed that the men stared at me, as the only woman in the group that walked in. I'm sure they didn't know what to think. They probably hadn't seen women carrying weapons. One man would not recognize me when I was introduced. We were with some trade officials and trying to facilitate the food system, and I went up to shake hands with some of them. He

refused, and although I continued to see him and interact with him many times, he avoided me or glared at me. He was not willing to accept that as military, I was not just a woman, but there to facilitate. Otherwise, most men were respectful.

I think it's how you carry yourself. They usually recognize rank. I'm a captain, and I think it's one thing they don't have in their army. The Iraqi Army was pretty much generals and corporals. I always dealt with them in a professional manner—"Here's what we've planned—here's what's going to happen," and I never got much trouble from them.

SSgt Pinedo remembers,

I had one incident during the election when an Iraqi working to facilitate the voting told me he didn't listen to women telling him what to do. So I told him, "Well, if you don't listen to me, then you're not going to get paid." It was as simple as that. No work, no pay.

He listened, but then balked at cleaning up his stuff after eating. It's still their country, so they are accustomed to making whatever mess they want, but they're in our camp, our area. I asked him to clean up after himself and he told me, "In my house, the women clean." I said, "This is my house, this is my camp, so the men clean their own mess." And he started picking it up. He got a little testy, but it worked.

LtCol Sarah Cope tells me about a time in her first deployment during 2003 when, as an MP, she was clearing buildings in Fallujah during an early assault.

The Iraqi families live in buildings clustered around a compound. I led the teams to clear, and once we got into the compound, I directed everybody from there. You'd bring everybody together into the compound, so I was securing a lot of people—a lot of women and children. Sometimes the women would smile, and they had a look that said I'd sparked their interest—especially the younger ones. It must have made them think there were other things women could do besides what they were doing. A couple of them wanted to talk with me when we had interpreters.

Cpl Brandie Collette, also an MP, works with transporting enemy prisoners of war (EPW) during her second deployment in Iraq. As convoy security, part of her job is to set up camps for male EPW and transport them from one detainment center to another.

"Were there no female detainees?" I ask.

"I've never handled female detainees. The women I've seen don't seem very aggressive toward anybody. They seem shy to me, like they don't really want to get involved. They stay in their homes when we're around. Sometimes they peek out at us because they're curious, but they won't approach me.

I facilitate getting the male detainees on and off the trucks. The blindfolds are off when I'm handling them. They act disgraced when I'm working with them. I didn't really notice at first because I'm just doing my job. But some of the Marines tell me they see the detainees walking with me with their heads down, shaking their heads. They feel disgraced because a female is touching their arm.

I'm proud of what I do. If the prisoner has done something bad, he deserves to be handled according to our rules, not his. Other than that, I haven't had anybody say anything to me directly. Once, in the city [Fallujah], some soldiers told me some of the Iraqi men were saying some pretty rude things about me being a female in the Marines, and the soldiers made them back off. I really didn't know what they were saying. I'm very different around Iraqi women. I think the way some of the women look at me, they're impressed, like "Wow, look at her." That's what I want them to think.

1stLt Alexandra Plucinski, a logistics officer, has also worked with detainees in the city of Fallujah, but as an officer, she sees a different response.

We're trained just like our male counterparts, and we have a job to do. At the same time, you're always conscious you're a female. Your hair's back, you're wearing all this body armor and your Kevlar—it conceals every part of physical recognition, so the Iraqis don't think I'm female. We're transporting detainees and my Marines have to load them into the trucks. I give my instructions to my Marines and the Iraqis hear my voice. They're blindfolded and cuffed, but even so you get the feeling they're shocked. "What is she doing? Why did this girl try to detain us when our hands aren't available?" One time we had two men who turned out just to have been at the wrong place at the wrong time, and they were cleared as innocent by the intelligence team. They were watching the others get loaded and I looked over and saw them gesturing—"What is this? Who are these people that allow their women to do this? How is it they have a woman to do this job? And in charge of the men?"

When we get to the Iraqi security forces, to turn them over, there's a mixture of harassment and disdain toward me from them, but some of them treat me just like anyone else. I make sure I'm as genderless as possible. I'm not easily intimidated, and I don't back away if they're coming at me. A few places we go, they'll start catcalling, yelling things, and laughing. A few have gotten too close and tried to touch my face. "What's your name?" I tell them, "You don't need to know. Get away from me!"

At times, I'll just walk off by myself. But at one of the Iraqi National Guard stations I walked away and a staff sergeant ran up to me, "You can't walk around by yourself. They're going to riot." I think he was exaggerating, but I don't like to think what the Iraqis might do. When we're on the road I have my M16 and two different knives with me. I almost decked one of them the other day. They were very insistent on getting in close to me. They kept coming and I told them, "Get away from me! Go away!" My male partner came over and by then I was yelling, "Get the fuck away from here, assholes, do you understand that?" They just laughed and walked away.

Now when I go out I often let my driver walk first and I'll follow five meters behind him. I just let him go ahead. Because the Iraqis take him seriously. It's their culture. When I see the Iraqi women I see that they're the ones doing the work, carrying all the loads. At one stop I had an Iraqi say to me in English, "You're so beautiful. We don't have women here like you." I tell them I have a job to do and to get away. They think it's funny. As for me, I don't feel it undermines my authority at all. They have to know that we're trained as much as the men are, and I'm sure they've had conversations among themselves, "Don't mess with them."

Fallujah, in 2005, two months after the city was secured and opened to the citizens for resettlement, is beginning to return to normal. There are markets opening, even though many of the storefronts were destroyed and windows smashed. There are pig carcasses hanging from the curtain of useless electric wires draped everywhere, sheep being herded through the streets, fresh produce, and bicyclists. Everywhere houses, shops, apartments, schools, and commercial buildings are under construction.

1stLt Sara Hope, who honchoed the formation of the Female Search Force, a group of volunteer women Marines trained to search Iraqi women who were reentering Fallujah for resettlement, found it "a little wild" to be working with the Iraqi military.

I have a better understanding of what the plan is [for resettling Fallujans], but I see what a different mind-set the Iraqi military has. We have to help them develop the right mind-set if they're going to be an effective force and then let them take over. They don't have NCO [noncommissioned officer] leadership like we do, so either they're officers or senior enlisted soldiers, or just soldiers, that's it. They don't take the initiative and responsibility for their troops yet. They fluff up their numbers intentionally so they can get more money, and then when we try to account for them it's a nightmare, because you don't really know how many soldiers they have. For us, accountability is the number one thing.

I'm not sure who sets their pay, but if they say, "Hey, we have 300 soldiers" and on the books they really have 250, then that x number of dollars for those 50 extra soldiers goes into the pockets of the officers. Or they can get food for that many people, and they can sell what they don't eat—that kind of stuff. I think it's just sort of an institutionalized thing for them. It's not wrong, to them. That's how they do business. So we're trying to break that. The Marines and soldiers that work directly with the Iraqis as liaisons, I think they probably have the most important and the most challenging job out here of anybody. It's a tough job. It's extremely important, though. They're doing a really good job.

Hope also has problems with Iraqi men respecting her rank as a Marine. When she was working with the Iraqi Police training her female searchers at checkpoints where they would work together, she was dogged with the Iraqi Police learning English phrases to say to the searchers. "You're beautiful" or "I love you" would drive the searchers crazy. Hope felt it was tolerable if they could laugh at it and it didn't get out of hand. But once an Iraqi policeman told Hope she was beautiful. Her Marine sergeant told the man, "You can't say that to her. She's a lieutenant." The Iraqi did not understand, so the sergeant said, "If you tell her she's beautiful, she'll make us do push-ups." The Iraqi said, "No, no, she can't make us do push-ups." And the sergeant said, "Yes, she can. She's an officer." The Iraqi wouldn't give up. "Well, maybe she can make me do push-ups, but not you." And the sergeant said, "Why not?" "Because she's an officer, but you're a man."

"They believed I was only an officer of female Marines," Hope says. "It never occurred to them that a woman could be in a place of authority over a man. But the sergeant set him straight."

Another problem area is paying Iraqis who work on the Marine bases. Cpl Michelle Garza, a Disbursing Clerk, says Thursday is payday for Iraqis; they are paid $7, in American money, a day. "Every group has a foreman," she says.

> We pay the foremen and they pay their workers. The American dollars are worth a lot to them. They always want new bills. At least ones that look new. If you give them an old dollar, an ugly dollar, they'll give it back to you to exchange. They can't trade the old dollars out there. It has to be in mint condition when we give it to them.
>
> Sometimes it's sad to see how these people live. I went to Camp Manhattan to disburse funds to laborers there. [Al Anbar Security College, which trains Iraqi Police, is located near Camp Manhattan. Its classrooms and dorms were built by independent contractors using Iraqi labor.] Some of the people I see are classy, wearing nice clothes. But others are in dirty, worn clothes. You realize that [even here] these people have a community, a mayor, some structure to their lives. There is an Iraqi family living in a house in Camp Manhattan, and I went there to make a payment. There was a woman and her six-month-old baby in the house—it is so different for them. It must be really tough.
>
> Iraqi men look at me weirdly at times. I don't offer my hand to them most of the time because I know it's disrespectful. But sometimes they look uncomfortable taking money from me, a female Marine. I'm there to pay them, so I don't really care. One man spoke really good English. He told me he needed an American wife. There are comments like that. And could they have me instead of the money. You tell them their government would get mad, but they say, no, American women are different. Sometimes they tell me they have five wives at home. It's crazy. But when they see me, they know me. I'm the money lady.

LtCol Cindy Atkins, who does accountability for the Marines, likens Iraq to a dysfunctional family.

I learned a lot about domestic violence, having been a Family Advocate Officer many times in my career in the Marine Corps. The Iraqis have been in a domestic violence relationship for 40 years. They don't know any better. They don't know that they don't have to be treated that way, that there is a better way to be treated, another way to live. All they know is that one day at a time we are helping them take little steps to realize that they deserve better.

For instance, they had Iraqi women running for office who were intimidated and had threats on their lives, and they continued to stand up and run. They're learning, slowly. They had a large number of Iraqi women turn out to vote in Fallujah, the largest number of women in the country, I think. That's a good sign. That, and the other day a Fallujan went to an Iraqi soldier to report insurgent activity in the neighborhood. They didn't approach the Marines. They went to their own people, the Iraqi soldier. They're taking the initiative to make a better life for themselves.

They need to trust their own forces. That's our goal. Right now they depend on us. They're not going to get there overnight, but they're going in the right direction. For people to do that, it's a huge step to taking back their own city.

A Marine I knew who was wounded has been training Iraqi soldiers. One of them became his training buddy, and he carried a photo of the Iraqi in his wallet. He told me that they still worry about how the Iraqi soldiers handle detainees. They tend to be a little harsh on the detainees. He said they had to intervene and tell them, "No, you can't do that. That's not how we treat them. You have to detain them under the Geneva Convention, that's how it's done." It's a pattern that's been set for them, being treated badly and we have to break that. That's our ticket home, to get those forces to stand up.

One evening the women Marine officers at Camp Fallujah invite me to join them at an Iraqi dinner in a convention hall on base. It is a considerable walk, and while the building is unimposing, the interior is quite elegant. There are banks of picture windows and a round conference table of shining, polished red wood, perhaps cherry, with comfortable, padded chairs around the edges. At the side, fronting a kitchen area, is a buffet counter with metal serving dishes piled high with Iraqi food—specially cooked for these women who gather once every few weeks to have a taste of the national fare—a break from the chow hall, and a chance to share a meal together. Waiting for the food to arrive, they watch TV almost in a trance, as they wind down after the long day. Eventually, the conversation gets animated and even raucous at times, as they eat, drink soft drinks, and share the odd, the special, the weird, the haunting, or meaningful moments of their work. It is a rare girl thing.

In the chow halls, I notice the foreign contractors working there, serving food, cleaning up. I wonder if they are Iraqi. I also wonder what they must think about the abundance and variety of food served in the cafeteria lines, when so many of their countrymen are barely surviving.

The chow halls are vast, serving upwards of 500 people at long tables. At the door, a Marine guard checks my credentials. There are long sinks with multiple spigots for everyone to wash their hands. Service is on paper plates. In the cafeteria lines for hot food you indicate what food you want by pointing, and the food workers load your plate. There are usually three meat choices, and fish, three kinds of potatoes, three hot veggies, rolls, pasta with sauce, bread, pizza, hotdogs, and hamburgers dished up on the spot. There is also a salad bar with iceberg lettuce and olives, mushrooms, croutons, tomatoes, carrots, beans, cheese, bacon bits, coleslaw, noodle salad, potato salad, and five or six dressings. There are boxed juices and juice dispensers. There are boxes of whole milk, skim milk, and half & half. Coke, Pepsi, Mountain Dew, and 7-Up bottled in Saudi Arabia are available, as are tea bags and hot water, brewed coffee, regular and decaf. For dessert there is ice cream, frozen fruit and fudge bars, fruit pies, pumpkin and pecan pies, cakes, three kinds of cheesecake, lemon bars, chocolate chip and butter cookies—and fresh fruit, usually kiwis, oranges, Jonathan and Pippin apples, grapes, and bananas. And there are bowls of trail mix.

It is like any American cafeteria, but I cannot help thinking about the enormous effort to get all that food into Iraq—the convoys that must be escorted by Marines and are often bombed or attacked with mortars. The Marines tell me that when there are days without fresh lettuce, for instance, everyone supposes it is because a convoy of semis was attacked. Nothing is too good for the military, as far as food is concerned. They often have steak and lobster nights. I think of the hundreds of trucks traveling the dangerous roads at night, taking all the delicacies to the bases, and all the Marine women I meet, the supply officers who order and inventory trillions of pounds of supplies, and the radio operators talking to the Marine convoys, the pilots who fly cargo planes, and the vehicle mechanics.

One Saturday evening at Camp Fallujah, I join the women Marine officers on a rooftop near our quarters for a late evening cigarette and for some, a private Saturday night libation. There are few lights on most of the base, and so everyone carries a personal red-filtered flashlight. Consequently, the conditions for stargazing are optimum. The Marines joke and laugh, unwinding and talking about personal matters—their families and events at home.

We have a clear view of the city of Fallujah, some four miles distant. Col Holbert remarks about how many more lights there are in the city each time they are up there on the roof. CWO Adamson points out what she thinks is new lighting at the power station.

Col Holbert remembers watching convoys approaching on the long road from Baghdad and the airport supply areas. The contractors drove the big resupply semis with lights on; the military vehicles were always blacked out. She recalls hearing military vehicles, not seeing them, especially the tanks. Their grinding treads were loud on the sand and across pavement. She would listen as they moved across the horizon. This was also the time she said evening prayers. "I felt very close to God out there in the desert. I prayed for peace to come to the country."

And then they begin to reminisce about the evenings, three months earlier, when they sat on the rooftop to watch the Battle of Fallujah in progress. They told me about watching a skyline that was a blaze of explosions, columns of smoke and flame, and hearing the deep booms and jarring sounds of battle. Then, they had been watching the city's near total destruction. Now, they are witnessing its rebirth. In the silence that settles on us I am overwhelmed by the surreal situation of my being in the war in Iraq, looking at the city of Fallujah, with these dynamic women warriors and their almost palpable memories.

5

WINNING HEARTS AND MINDS

At 1930 hours, after a standard 14-hour shift, six Marines, arriving back at their base in Camp Fallujah, are looking forward to some chow, a hot shower, and maybe five hours of sleep. They are told there has been a request for an interview by a writer, and they agree to do it. I understand these are no ordinary Marines, and the Marines are told this is no ordinary writer.

Ranging in age from 20 to 28, these Marines are part of the volunteer Female Search Force (FSF) that has been operating at the gates to the city of Fallujah since it reopened to its citizens after the devastating Battle of Fallujah in November 2004. They are curious as to why anyone would want to talk to them and are also interested to have a look at me.

It is already dark when Lt Gilbert, my Public Affairs escort, and I meet them coming across the field as we cut through a gate in the adobe wall into the outer area of the camp, heading to the media tent. Gilbert greets them and they fall in with us. They are used to the uneven rubble and hard sand of the camp and trudge through the darkness looking back to see if I am keeping up.

There is a growing moon that throws gray shapes of tents around us into black relief against the sand. It is too dark to distinguish any faces under the Kevlar helmets. We are not sure which tent is our destination, so Lt Gilbert lifts the tent flap of one to peer into the darkness, finding only cots. The next tent is the one. We climb the wooden steps and go in, securing the tent flaps behind us, and turn on the harsh overhead fluorescent light. The tent has a wood floor and is empty except for benches and tables. There are American-style electrical connections here for the media to plug in their laptops and cell phone chargers. There is no Internet available unless the reporters have satellite connections. There is a large heating and cooling unit in the corner run by a generator outside. The clamorous roar from the generator causes me some concern in regard to taping this session, but the time these Marines have given me is precious —I'll have to make the best of it.

The Marines assure Lt Gilbert they will escort me back to the Public Affairs Office. It is on the way to the chow hall. So Gilbert leaves and we look each other over.

Digital camouflage uniforms hide the dust and sweat of a long day in the city. They remove their Kevlar helmets and heavy flak vests, and their hair is slicked back, still neatly caught in a bun at the nape of their necks, or boyishly short. They wear green T-shirts under their field cammies. Two have .9mm pistols strapped to their thighs; the others carry their M16s with the black strap across their chests, muzzle pointed down toward the floor.

We seat ourselves at benches in a semicircle around the digital recorder I have laid on the bench in the center of the room; to address their curiosity, I give them some background on who I am and why I am there. These women look wary and exhausted and for once, I want to seem like "mom" to put them at ease.

These are enlisted Marines—two are sergeants, the others corporals and lance corporals. They are Sgt Erin Black, Sgt Lori B. Luna, LCpl Alicia D. Waters, Cpl Stephanie N. Little, Cpl Stephanie Ullman, and Cpl Rebecca Ann (Becky) Brooks. They have engaging smiles and marvelously white teeth. Under other circumstances they could be a volleyball team or friends having lunch at the mall. No one wants to begin the conversation by talking about herself. Finally I ask one of them to tell me her name, rank, and MOS. Slowly, as she begins to answer my nonpolitical questions there are smiles, and then a spontaneous interjection of agreement or a wry comment. In no time we are all laughing, and I am showing my obvious amazement at their stories.

These Marines are all volunteers for the Female Search Force, a unit created especially by the Marine Corps to deal with a unique situation: How can Marines search civilian Iraqis, which they intend to do with returning Fallujans, when Muslim women cannot be touched by any male other than their husbands or close relatives? Even taking a woman by the arm to assist or lead her is cause for alarmed shouting and a rush of male anger and indignation. "Winning hearts and minds" is what the Marines say motivated them to recruit women Marines for FSF.

The FSF receives as much as six weeks of training in basic Arabic greetings and commands and in searching techniques. The unit was put together as the Battle of Fallujah—Al Fajr—was winding down and the Marines turned from being warriors to humanitarians—a role new to them but something they really get into. In a city originally of about 285,000, nearly 80 percent of the structures in Fallujah were partially or completely destroyed during the battle or by air strikes before the

Marines went in. The continued resistance of insurgents using tunnels and spider holes to attack the Marines by surprise dogged progress by Marine Civil Affairs, Navy Seabees, and engineering groups working to restore city services, make assessments of damage, and repair power grids. More of the city was destroyed as Marines continued to find weapons caches. They had to blow them in place rather than evacuate the ordnance out to an open field to destroy all the weapons. Caches are routinely booby-trapped to explode when touched. Sometimes, Marines would find weapons caches in buildings they had searched the day before. The citizens, who had almost entirely evacuated Fallujah before the battle, would return when the Iraqi Interim Government and the Marines could guarantee their safety and control entry to the city.

While the search for insurgents continued, the FSF Marines trained in use of communication equipment, defensive techniques, convoy rehearsals, Arabic history, and customs. Cpl Stephanie Ullman, of Wausau, Wisconsin, says,

> We were taught how to take a woman to the ground if needed, and to remove weapons or suicide bombs if they were found during a search. Each ECP (Entry Control Point) had its own call sign and we could reach any of the other checkpoints over a PRC-119 (portable radio case).

LCpl Alicia Waters and Sgt Erin Black, as Military Police, had already had much of the training for restraining or searching and so helped to train other FSF members while waiting for the city to open. LCpl Waters has an ear for language and picked up quite a bit of Arabic in addition to the basic commands taught the searchers. "You'd be surprised how much you can learn if you just listen," she says.

> I think the Iraqi women really appreciated the fact that we took the time to learn some of their language. They would say, "Oh, you know Arabic?" It made them happy. I thought that seeing me as a woman in a position of power, that knowledge made them feel good about themselves as women.

Cpl Becky Brooks, also an MP, and a K9 Dog Handler, considered the "decent amount of Arabic" she learned essential in searching the Iraqi women and their belongings, as well as the vehicles her dog searched.

> With the women, it made them more at ease. They were already uncomfortable, and when we could tell them what we needed them to do in their own language, it simplified everything. A typical day for us, as searchers, was 14 to 15 hours at the checkpoints and travel time. Some of us had shorter or longer days; for instance, with the dogs, we could only search a couple of hours at a time and then we would rotate out and I would help the searchers with the Iraqi women. I carried an M9 because my M16 could get in the way of my dogs when they're searching vehicles.

LCpl Waters tells me,

Most of the searchers stayed at the same checkpoint. I moved to different checkpoints so I could help train new searchers. The last checkpoint I worked was on the bridge where the Blackwater contractors were killed and their bodies strung up. That checkpoint is very small and normally has two searchers and four male Marines.

SSgt Gianniana Pinedo is another FSF member I speak with in a separate interview. She talks about searching a few women who were extremely well-dressed,

like you might see in Baghdad. When we searched them we had them raise their scarves, and many were wearing makeup and were very pretty. That's the reason their husbands want to cover them up. But most of the women are poor and look like bag ladies. Their purses are full of junk—paper nightgowns that are sold on the base, clothes, or socks. And I would say 80 percent of the women coming through are pregnant. Sometimes they have 10 or 11 kids, and still they're pregnant. Sometimes they had a really big, tight belly and I'd say, "Baby?" and they'd shake their head "No." They were just fat.

When we leave the media tent an hour or so later, these six women walk me home, bantering about how they have been thinking of writing to Oprah to try to get on her show to tell their story. "I'll bet I can do that for you," I suggest. They laugh and joke about how they would dress on the show—like women, or Marines. They all think it would be fabulous to get a makeover. I tell them I will keep in touch and let them know if Oprah is interested in what they are doing. When I return to the States, I e-mail the program staff at Oprah about the extraordinary things these women are doing in Iraq. At the time, Oprah was producing a series of stories about American teen girls and the problems and successes they have. I suggest that these FSF women, most of them barely out of their teens themselves, are a sobering but educative contrast to the teens she is interviewing here in the States. Oprah does not bite, although I pursue it for the next couple of months. This is disappointing, but is indicative of the general disconnect of the country with the war and the lack of human interest stories coming from Iraq.

Not receiving word from Oprah's staff, I also contact Katie Couric, Diane Sawyer, and other newswomen, but to no avail. There is no interest, it would seem, in military women so far away from the public consciousness. Four months after I return from Iraq, these women have rotated out of Iraq and the women Marines they trained for replacement are deliberately targeted, one evening, by a suicide bomber who aims his vehicle at the truck carrying them out of the city to return to Camp Fallujah. Three Marines of the FSF are killed along with one woman Seabee, and 13 women are wounded in a holocaust of flame that destroys their seventon vehicle as well as two Humvees escorting them. This gets the attention of the media. But the reports of the incident are cursory, with little explanation as to what their role was and why they were targeted. I write John Burns, the *New York Times* bureau chief in Baghdad at the time, to compliment him on his comprehensive reporting of the incident, giving a more meaningful picture of who the women were and what they were doing in Fallujah. He responds with some surprise that I was there interviewing their predecessors, and we exchange e-mails about the possibility of interviewing one or two of the six women I interviewed. But within hours, another, more compelling incident terminates interest in the horrific attack on the FSF. The terribly burned and disfigured Marines are transported, eventually, to Brooke Army Medical Center in San Antonio. Some take as long as a year, undergoing excruciating treatment, to heal.

When 1stLt Sara Emond Hope, administrative adjutant, first heard about the idea of forming the Female Search Force, she let her commanding officer and her higher headquarters know that she definitely wanted to be considered.

> I knew they weren't going to be able to let too many officers do it, so I wanted to get my foot in the door. For three weeks I begged and pleaded and promised not to let any of my other duties slide. I'd still do the admin and all that. So they made me OIC (Officer-in-Charge) of the detachment.
>
> We had no idea how many [female volunteers] we were going to be getting, or when we were going to get them. They were coming from all over Iraq, all the different Marine bases around here. Eventually we had our full load, 20 altogether. We had 2 soldiers and 18 Marines, all different MOS, lance corporal, corporal, and sergeant. It was a dynamic group. We had some time to kill because they kept putting off the opening of the city, so we filled it with as much training as we could get done. And they went to the range and fired AK-47s, and did martial arts.
>
> We trained in nonlethal takedowns, which is a manipulation with arm bars, basically police-type stuff—everything but shooting your weapon. Even though the rules of engagement are clear about when you can shoot and when you can't shoot, we were going to be near women and children, so we wanted to make sure we had all that covered.

The Rules of Engagement are clear to Marines at all times, but examples specific to the theater of operations are necessary so they know that if they have to fire, it is legal, in regard to the Geneva Convention.

> They opened Fallujah on December 23rd, so on the 22nd we did a rehearsal and sent everyone out to the sites they were going to be working so they would understand how they operated. On the 23rd we launched out there. We would search all day long. We didn't search at all entry checkpoints, for instance, the contractor entry sites, because we didn't anticipate a lot of females coming through there. We just went to the sites that would have the most Iraqi civilians coming through them.

The psyops [psychological operations] guys would go out with their loud-speakers on Humvees and drive to other cities and announce that Fallujah would be open on the 23rd. The first couple of days were really slow, but then it really started to pick up. At each site, probably on average, we were seeing 200, 300 women and children a day. Then it died down for a while. The weather got bad. Then when it picked back up, there were upwards of 1,600 to 1,800 women and children a day.

Some checkpoints would have heavier vehicle traffic, some heavier foot traffic. The Iraqi Police were the ones that searched the men. So if there were female Iraqi Police, there wouldn't be a need for us. The women would come in through a separate walkway in the actual control point. At one point we'd take over and guide them over to our area. The search areas were private, cordoned off. We'd have one person searching and one person to form the lines and provide a sense of control over the whole thing, because sometimes we had very large groups of women waiting.

The lines were long. At the vehicle checkpoints, sometimes people would tell us the Iraqis were waiting in their cars for six or seven hours. In the other search lines, women sometimes waited two or three hours. At other times, the lines for women would go so much more quickly than the men that the women would laugh at their husbands. The women would come in, go get things from the site of their houses, go put them in their car outside the checkpoint or drop it off somewhere and come back in. We'd see some of them three, four, five times a day, just going through the lines, while their husbands were waiting in line or were working at the home sites.

We figured most of the families were going back out at night, because there wasn't any water or power, and it was still pretty cold. We thought they were going in, cleaning out, trying to figure out what to do with their things, helping their neighbors, things like that. Before the city was opened it was totally empty. There was nothing, nobody there. Now the city is coming back. It's an amazing thing to see. The atmosphere now is that the Americans are doing a good job keeping the city secure. When the Iraqis see something that's not right, they're much more inclined to tell an Iraqi soldier or an Iraqi police officer and they know we'll go address it. If they tell us where there are weapons, they know we'll go and get them, so they're not frightened or afraid of retribution like they might otherwise be.

1stLt Hope tells me they got a lot of their search techniques from LCpl Waters and Sgt Black, MPs who had been doing searches at the detention facility.

It's done by the book, by the numbers. But we found that once we got out there, we didn't really have to have the women put their hands on their heads. These are pretty feeble women we're dealing with—large, but feeble. And we didn't want to lose any hearts and minds. So they use their best judgment.

We were looking primarily for weapons, anything that was suspicious, wires, devices for building bombs, things that were hidden, but also large sums of money, fake IDs, and cell phones. The cell phones we'd turn over to intel and they'd do their thing, then give them back. We didn't keep them. They're allowed to have cell phones.

We only detained one woman the entire time [in two months prior to the interview] because she had several passports with the same photo and different names. When they questioned her, they found out that her brother, who she came into the city with, had the same thing. You get a feeling, working with the women every day, what's suspicious and what's not. There was a lot of intel at the time that the Mujahideen were going to try to use a female suicide bomber to disrupt our operations. So we made sure everybody was aware of what to look for.

Searchers had M16s and would face the women. There would be a cover person that was always armed, so they'd be behind in case someone reached for the searcher's M16. That could be dangerous. Wearing a firearm wasn't a problem, on your thigh or underarm. We were always on guard and always vigilant, but if you could see these women, it's really hard to feel threatened by them. Mostly they are just scared. I do think they were definitely appreciative. You could see the change from when they came in initially and their reaction was fear—they were crying and shaking. They thought we were men leading them away from their husbands and they didn't want to go. They'd freak out. We would take off our Kevlar [helmets] and let them see our hair, and sometimes even wear our hair down out of our Kevlar so they could see it. Once they saw that we were women, too, their faces just lit up and they were so happy. It's hard for us to understand—but for them to be touched by someone other than their husband or father—it's a big deal to them. So they were very pleased. Then there were some who had attitudes. They didn't think they should be searched and they told us so. Most were very pleased and appreciative. After a time, they'd try to give us food and tip us. They'd always shake our hands. We allow that sometimes. We'd exercise our judgment. To see what these people have been through—obviously some could be supporting the enemy, but when you see the women every day, you kind of develop a rapport with them. You just hope everything works out for them.

We noticed that the Iraqi policemen were just as happy to let us take the women off to the side to be searched. The women in large crowds could be pushy and irritable. But to be honest, the men are kind of weak when it comes to women. When we'd see some woman who would say she was too sick to get out of the car to be searched, her male Iraqi companion would say, "Okay, stay in the car." So we'd have to reach in and pull them out. "No, you have to get out." I found the IP [Iraqi Police] a little lazy, and they wouldn't stand up to an Iraqi woman even if it was part of their job. But they're getting better. They're learning a lot.

It has been a long day for the FSF. Cpl Ullman recounts,

I'd get up at 0415 to make sure I had time to eat chow before heading out to the city. The convoy usually left at daybreak, around 0530. On average we'd return to camp by 1900, but there were many nights when we didn't make it back until 2200. Then we'd come home and shower and get some chow and hit the rack to do it all over again the next day. We would get one day off a week to do laundry and make a PX run.

I thought the majority of the Iraqi women appreciated the fact that we were there to ensure their safety. They saw all our efforts to keep weapons, drugs, and contraband out of the city and understood we were doing it for them.

The Marines of the 4th Civil Affairs Group (CAG) work with Iraqi women to establish the sorts of community organizations commonly found everywhere in the United States. LtCol Cope, an MP who was also a police officer as a civilian and escorted troop convoys during the war in 2003, is attached to 4th CAG; she tells me that when they arrived in September 2004 (her second deployment in Iraq, but first with CAG) they noticed that the Marines were dealing with only the Iraqi men while on foot patrols in the communities.

They didn't have the ability to work with the women and children. So we all began talking and put together what's called a Female Information and Operations Civil Affairs Team [FIOCA]. It was a group of us who got together to figure out how to start dealing with the other 50 to 60 percent of this country. It was a team of all females. We started out going to the female venues out west in Al Anbar province. There are a lot of all-female venues. We began setting up sewing shops in different places. They say the men run everything, but it's the women who run everything. They just do it behind the scenes. They're the ones who are kicking their husbands out to construct IEDs [for pay] so they can have money, or they keep their husbands in because they don't want them killed. They raise the children up to the age of 14 or 15 and then the men take over. So they're the future of this country. Because of all the wars they've had, the men keep getting knocked off. I don't think the program we put together has enough emphasis yet because there're just not a lot of female Marines over here. If we had volunteers for a female team of officers and headquarters element, you'd have to convince someone else to let their people go [from their assigned jobs] for a short time in order to be able to do it. I believe this country would go a long way if they started concentrating on the 50 percent that they're ignoring—the females.

LtCol Cope tells me that one of the female interpreters they use has told her that she is amazed that Americans pay so much attention to Iraqi cultural issues, particularly women's issues. Obviously, it has not been of major importance in Iraqi culture. Cope says,

I think that the women are highly underestimated here. I don't care if they're from the far west and wear burkas every day, they are also very intelligent and they know what's going on in their surroundings and they want their families alive and well. Now, they're still focused on survival. They're focused on feeding their family and getting their lives back to normal, especially in Fallujah. I think they're hopeful about democracy. That's why so many showed up to vote.

The city is very antiquated. Saddam did nothing for them here. The water filtration system for Fallujah was terrible. They dump all their raw sewage and waste in the water and let the water sit, all the junk falls to the bottom, they sift the water off the top and they drink it. We have introduced the idea of a water filtration system similar to what we have in the States—something that really cleans the water. And the electrical wiring was unbelievable. They'd swipe wiring from anywhere and it's just a hodgepodge.

The deteriorating utility infrastructure was evident in the city long before the military arrived in Fallujah. Electricity was routinely stolen from connections, resulting in giant cobwebs of wires strung everywhere, some only 3 to 4 feet off the ground.

They use all kinds of different fuels—benzene, kerosene, diesel. The problem is, there's plenty of oil in this country but only one place to process it, so there's generally a shortage. Saddam put all his money into palaces. He didn't put it into building his country and providing his people the services they needed to get by. There's a telephone system, there are land lines—but they're mainly going wireless which is probably the way things will continue.

There's a humanitarian assistance site where the women come to pick up clothes, food, and water. The women come through several times in a day.

The food distributed at these sites is international MREs (Meals Ready-To-Eat), specifically for use by any ethnic group—made with beef, chicken, or lamb (no pork products). They are distributed by USAID (U.S. Agency for International Development—a program developed in the Kennedy administration) in connection with the U.S. military.

SSgt Gianniana Pinedo says it is ridiculous to wonder why they are not more concerned about their future.

Their future is the next day. They can't plan much beyond that. If you look at it, there are some of the same things still happening to them that happened under Saddam. People still come in their homes in the middle of the night if we get intel that there's something going on.

LtCol Cope continues,

We still do raids, and searches. We're still tracking down caches. If it's not us, it's the bad guys. There's always the possibility of someone showing up at their house. If they work with the Coalition forces, the Muj [Mujahideen] find out and they disappear. If they work with the Muj, we take them. So there's still a lot of things to keep them from focusing too far out in the future. They just want to be able to wake up the next day in the same place. They're still wondering if they're going to have water and if they can find food for the family somewhere. That's Fallujah, and further west they have the same issues.

Civil Affairs also established the Civil-Military Operations Center (CMOC) in Fallujah, one of many centers established all over Iraq to facilitate assistance for local Iraqis. They may need identity cards or solatia (condolence) payments for damage to their houses from the battle or loss of life or injury of a family member—humanitarian assistance.

CWO4 Kim Adamson, who is a civil court judge in civilian life, has taken that experience to Iraq, applying it to the fledgling judicial system. She works with the courts in Fallujah. Explaining the CMOC, she says,

> It's a gathering place for meetings and a place to coordinate reconstruction and infrastructure repair projects specific to the city. The Marines work there with the local population, the Sheiks, the tribal leaders, the municipality heads, department heads. They're trying to rebuild, to get schools opened. There was a lot of damage in the city. We're not doing the work for them. We position ourselves so that we can enable them. The Iraqi people do it themselves. It would do them no good if we just came in and did everything and say, "There, that's done." People realize the value of what they have if they build it themselves. We help them devise plans, find funding, hire workers.
>
> As the Judicial Officer on the Fallujah Municipal Support team, I was tasked with starting a dialogue with the Fallujah judges and getting the Fallujah courthouse back in operation. The Fallujah courthouse had a lot of bomb damage and the majority of judges had fled the city prior to Operation Al Fajr [the Battle of Fallujah]. I communicated with judicial representatives at all levels, nation and provincial, either in person or through an intermediary, to get the Fallujah judges to return and meet with me at the Civil-Military Operations Center in downtown Fallujah following Al Fajr. It took several months, but eventually, a Fallujah Family Court Judge came into the CMOC, as well as the Fallujah Criminal Court Judge. The Criminal Court Judge and I visited the bombed-out courthouse, and I was able to get the funding to rebuild the courthouse, as well as six other courthouses in Al Anbar province.
>
> Every week, 4th CAG hosted the Fallujah Reconstruction Meeting at the CMOC. This was attended by many senior Iraqi and Coalition military, Iraqi ministerial level representatives, and local Fallujah municipal representatives, to include tribal Sheiks, former politicians, and other religious representatives. Discussions were oftentimes heated, but at least there was a face-to-face communication taking place. It was at one of these meetings where the Fallujah Family Judge spoke so eloquently. It was really quite moving. He spoke of how things were in the kingdom before Saddam Hussein; he quoted President Kennedy and spoke of the U.S. Civil Rights Movement. He was a forward thinker and had great hopes and aspirations for Iraq in a post-Saddam Hussein world. They couldn't have had this sort of conversation before. These are very smart and articulate people.

Adamson admits to a qualified optimism about the new government for Iraq. She expresses worries about the length of time it will take to stand up the government and then how it will carry on without our troops providing security.

Cpl Brandie Collette, who, as an MP, transported detainees, also is part of convoys into the city carrying water, blankets, and food to the resettling inhabitants. "We've also taken in toys for the children, and candy."

The Marine Corps also gave each Iraqi family $200 in American money from its own funds to get them started on rebuilding, without having to wait for payments from the Department of Defense or the Iraqi government. These payments were needed immediately, to keep the Iraqi families stable, while Iraqi and American red tape was worked through.

Capt Jennifer Morris is a Communications Officer whose MOS has changed somewhat in the command in Iraq. She is now in Information Operations—trying to figure out how to get through to the Iraqi people and get them to cooperate with the American forces, not with the insurgents.

We're trying to find different ways to communicate with that target audience. It involves intel, which interests me a lot. There are a lot of cultural experts here which help us think about the situation in other ways than the American point of view. We ask the experts, "If we put this message out on a poster in town, or handed it out at a checkpoint, would they respond to it positively? Would it make sense to them?" One thing we've really started to do is reach out to the women. A lot of mothers have sons and husbands and brothers involved in the insurgency, and we feel they must have some influence over them. So we've made a lot of products that say, "Mothers of Fallujah, do you want this for your sons?" and show a picture of a house that is rubble or an injured boy. "Or do you want this?" and the kid's smiling and going to school. We put a lot of that out there and it's been good. They've responded positively.

We have psyop teams that go into town and interact with the people. They talk face-to-face with them and hand them product [leaflets]. And they'll come back and give us reports. "Today we went out and they ripped up all our product. They didn't even want to talk to us. They avoided us." Or they'll tell us, "They came out of their houses and actually sought us out. They were smiling and waving at us and invited us in for tea."

Sometimes the response from the Iraqi people depends on how strong the insurgents have a hold on them. In Fallujah, the insurgents had really intimidated them to the point where they didn't want to be seen interacting with us even if they like us. We've seen towns change back and forth depending on the level of intimidation in that area.

In November, before the battle for the city, we were only on the outskirts, but we heard reports that the people were terrified. They were afraid to talk to their neighbors and would rat anyone out. So it was a mess. Once we started letting people back in, after we cleared the city, we were afraid they would be angry because their town was almost completely destroyed. But they weren't. It was surprising. We had people tell us, "Thank you for ridding the town of insurgents. My house is a pile of stones now, but it's going to be better." There are a lot of forces patrolling in and around the town now, and they feel safe. We've had reports that Iraqis have said, "This is the safest town in Iraq. I can't remember feeling this happy before." I mean, they have nothing. But they feel safe and that seems to be the most important thing.

The women seem to seek out female Marines. I was in a small village with a patrol and the women and girls were hiding behind the buildings, and the men were doing all the negotiating and dealing with the male Marines. The little children were running around being given toys and school supplies. The only females among the Marines were me and a translator. A kid came up to us and said to the translator, "The women want to talk to her." So the translator and I went to a corner of the building where we could be seen by the Marines, but they couldn't see who we were talking to. The women were so impressed, touching me and my uniform. They were saying thank you and filling up a big bag with dates to give me. They were getting ready for Ramadan, and so they had a lot of dates to make sweets. They told me, "The Sheik is so mean. All those school supplies you've given the children he will take away from the girls so only the boys can have them." That surprised us. It seemed they were opening up and telling us things the Marines would never hear from the Sheik.

Capt Morris has ambivalent feelings about how well the problems are being addressed.

I have days when I think *one step forward, three steps back.* And other days I'm convinced we're making a difference, slowly but surely. Some of my friends who are at the battalion level pretty much interact in a particular town, and they have a much more positive outlook. They can see the changes, especially over the past six months. That continuity is good. It's harder to be up at this level and see how everything's going in the big picture.

One of my friends was assigned to patrol a little town and he said when they first got there, no one came out and nobody talked because people were getting their heads chopped off right and left. Kids couldn't go to school. Nobody went to work. They just stayed cooped up in their houses. His company patrolled aggressively and eventually drove the insurgents out. Then the insurgents would mortar the town from the outskirts. Eventually, the Marines killed them or drove them away altogether, and slowly but surely people came out and started being friendly to the Marines and the Iraqi military patrolling with the Marines. Next thing you know, kids are back in school. Now the Marines get invited to dinner all the time at people's houses. They love the Marines. They don't want them to leave. But that might not be a good thing. We want to leave one day.

"We're trying to bolster national pride," Capt Morris tells me—something Saddam had no use for before. He was the only hero.

On election day, there was an Iraqi policeman working one of the checkpoints. He saw a guy come up who acted suspiciously, like he might have a suicide belt on. When the guy pushed him away and started running toward the election hall, the Iraqi policeman chased him down, tackled him, and they blew up together, along with several people. We called him a hero. This man is a hero. He risked his life and saved other lives.

Another Iraqi, a lieutenant colonel in the Iraqi Army, was working in Fallujah last year when the Coalition government assigned Iraqi forces to police the area. He wasn't corrupt. He tried to convince his fellow Iraqis to work with the multinational forces. "They're here to help us. Let's cooperate. It's for the best." He was doing a lot of good, and then one day he got kidnapped. He was tortured, and they cut his head off and left his body outside Fallujah. Either the State Department or the Iraqi government paid a large fee to his family as a condolence, and we put up a billboard outside the city to commemorate him. He's another hero. It's important to see that heroes are not forgotten. When we have people who work with us, their lives are in danger—there are other people willing to turn them in for money.

I ask Capt Morris how they can overcome this pattern with so many insurgents hidden among the cities and in the countryside.

Now that the elections are over, we see that the average Joe Iraqi is seeing that the insurgents, the jihadists, the foreign fighters who come in from Syria and other places are bringing nothing but more violence. They haven't opened a school. They haven't helped rebuild the town. They give the Iraqi citizens nothing. They just bring more destruction. I think they're starting to realize that. We've seen, again and again, in our interaction with the locals, less of a degree of support for the insurgency. They may be too afraid to help us, but they won't support the insurgents. We have to keep that attitude alive. They're the majority. They have to help push the bad guys out. If the insurgents don't have the cooperation of the townspeople, they can't operate. There have been incidents where the townspeople fight back. Sometimes they'll take up arms and fire on the insurgents if they see them setting something up. It's a situation where, "Hey, you're firing mortars at the Americans. They're going to fire back, and it could destroy my house." We want them to start protecting themselves.

It might take a generation before we see people feeling strong about their own protection. They could never do that before. Our translators tell us that things are much better than before, that there's more freedom already. I met an Iraqi journalist out here who worked at his paper for 30 years and was afraid all the time. He couldn't talk on his phone because it was bugged, and everything he wrote was censored. Now he says it's a free press—the only free press in all of the Middle East.

Now the Iraqis have access to so much more information. It only took six or seven months after Baghdad fell and half the houses sprouted satellite dishes on their roofs. They're getting channels from Lebanon and Egypt, and they have music videos. The women in Baghdad are starting to dress again in more Western fashions. We hope the children will see what other countries have and want that for themselves.

In the villages, the local Sheiks still have everybody under their thumb. It's a lot less progressive. There are women in the villages that have never seen a doctor because the doctors are men. They may have simple things, like infections, that could be easily treated, but they're left untreated and end up sterile, or whatever. We're working on education, but combat operations get in the way now and then. I know Lieutenant Colonel Cope told you about the Civil Affairs team we have out here for women's issues. We're trying to give them medical care, education, and set up centers where they can get job skills. But then combat operations may take over—they're going after insurgents—and we can't get back to the village for three months. It's going to take a long time.

The Public Affairs office, Camp Fallujah, Iraq. L-R: Cpl Mark Sixbey, Col Jenny Holbert, Sara Sheldon, MSgt Kelly Ramsey, LCpl Carrasco, Maj Francis Piccoli, and SSgt Garcia.

CWO4 Kim T. Adamson at Camp Fallujah.

LtCol Cindy Atkins.

Capt Amy B. Alger outside her office billet at Camp Taqqadum.

Cpl Terianne Anderson at Camp Taqqadum.

1stSgt Connie P. Arline.

SSgt Alison D. Arnold.

Female Search Force (FSF). 1st Row L-R: Cpl Rebecca A. Brooks, Sgt Erin Black, Sgt Lori B. Luna; 2nd Row L-R: Cpl Stephanie L. Ullman, LCpl Alicia D. Waters, and Cpl Stephanie N. Little at media tent, Camp Fallujah.

1stLt Blanca Binstock outside the officers' quarters, Camp Fallujah.

1stSgt Laura L. Brown in her office, Camp Taqqadum.

Cpl Brandie L. Collette at Camp Fallujah.

LtCol Sarah R. Cope.

Cpl Michelle P. Garza, with the chow hall in the far background, Camp Taqqadum.

LCpl Crystal L. Groves.

LCpl Mary K. Heathcoat outside her quarters at Camp Taqqadum.

Col Jenny M. Holbert in the patio behind the Public Affairs Office.

1stLt Sara E. Hope at Camp Fallujah.

The author and SgtMaj Suzanne R. How, with troop tents at TQ in the background.

2ndLt Samantha M. Kronschnabel at Camp Fallujah.

Capt Amy E. Malugani outside the base library, Camp Taqqadum.

Capt Jennifer B. Morris.

SSgt Gianniana Pinedo.

1stLt Alexandra Plucinski.

1stLt Anna V. Reves in the Public Affairs Office, Camp Taqqadum.

LtCol Loretta E. Reynolds at the Communications Battalion, Camp Fallujah.

1stLt. Tara A. Russell at Camp Taqqadum.

Capt Jodie L. Sweezey.

GySgt Amanda M. Vargas at her desk at Camp Taqqadum.

The author and Col Jenny M. Holbert at the entrance to Camp Fallujah.

Marine women with visiting senators at Camp Fallujah, L-R: Capt Jaden Kim, Senator Hillary Clinton, CWO4 Kim T. Adamson, 1st Sgt Irene O'Neal, LtCol Sarah R Cope, MSgt Kelly Ramsey, Capt Jennifer B. Morris, Senator Susan Collins, Col Jenny M. Holbert, LtCol Cindy Atkins, and Cpl Stephanie L. Ullman.

6

WOMEN IN COMBAT

While I am embedded at Camp Fallujah, five U.S. senators arrive on a visit with only a few hours' notice. Col Jenny Holbert, Public Affairs director for the Marines in Al Anbar province, assisted with special arrangements to provide a luncheon meeting for the senators with Marines from their home states. I tag along. There is only one reporter observing their visit to Fallujah—from the New York *Daily News*. Presumably, they held a formal press conference in Baghdad, so none of the news media had to follow them here to Fallujah.

A small room adjacent to the enormous chow hall is set up for the luncheon. It is a white-tiled room with a long wall with high windows, and there are tables that accommodate 12 to 14 people. There are five tables, each with a dozen enlisted Marines from each of the five states the senators represent: New York, Maine, Wisconsin, Arizona, and South Carolina. The senators are, respectively, Hillary Clinton, Susan Collins, Russ Feingold, John McCain, and Lindsey Graham.

The Marines are seated at attention, the straps of their M16s across their chests, muzzles, in many cases, touching the floor. The tables are decorated with a special paper tablecloth, the usual condiments, and a premade sandwich on white bread wrapped in plastic on a plate in front of each Marine. There is a lovely buffet along the side wall with varieties of meats, cheeses, breads, fruits, soft drinks and fruit juices, salads, and packages of chips. The Marines do not talk and do not move. They are in stunned awe at having the opportunity to meet their state senators. I remark to Col Holbert that I think it should be the other way around.

For the Marines asked to meet their senators, it is a welcome break from their work. Undoubtedly, thoughts of not screwing up and of having something special to call home about are uppermost in their minds.

I recognize Cpl Ullman sitting at the end of one table. She is one of the Female Search Force I interviewed two days earlier. I greet her and ask her how she has been selected to sit in on this luncheon session with

Senator Feingold; she says she has no idea. I later find she had been selected partly because of being awarded a commendation during Combat Training. Although women Marines go through combat training, they are, by law, prohibited from occupying positions that place them in combat and from actually taking part in combat.

All Marines receive Combat Training, men and women alike. Recruit training—taking a raw recruit through 13 weeks of boot camp and, upon graduation, pronouncing them Marines, is segregated training. Recruits are trained on both coasts—at San Diego and at Parris Island in South Carolina. This training is, according to the Marine Corps, "meant to transform civilians into Marines." All women recruits are trained at Parris Island separately from male recruits. They have female drill sergeants.

Combat Training for Marines follows boot camp, and the mission is to train all noninfantry Marines in the infantry skills required to operate in a combat environment. Male Marines are trained in the West at Camp Pendleton and in the East at Camp Lejeune, North Carolina. All women are trained in combat at Camp Lejeune. Combat Training for Marine infantry is 57 days long. For noninfantry, and all women, the program is 22 days.

Combat Training for women includes basic infantry tasks including use of various weapons, marksmanship, how to operate in environments contaminated by nuclear, biological, or chemical weapons, military operations in an urban area, and proper handling of prisoners of war. Combat Training instructors are both men and women Marines, and platoons of women Marines are often paired with their male counterparts in Combat Training. After Combat Training, women Marines go to their MOS schools—located in many different parts of the country.

As I chat with a group of some 15 female Marine officers who have come to observe the senators, many of whom I have interviewed, I remark to Col Holbert that it does not seem fair that out of the five senators arriving, two are women, whereas of the 60 Marines selected to meet their senators, only one is a woman. A little over 6 percent of the Marine Corps, currently at about 178,000 Marines, is female, or about 11,000. To have a comparable representation of female Marines at the luncheon meeting, three women could have been chosen. Or to equal the percentage of women senators, 24 women Marines might have been invited. But, these are definitely civilian observations. The Public Affairs Office had scant warning of the VIP visit, and there was no time to deal with such considerations.

The senators are considerably late in arriving, so the Marines are temporarily dismissed to go into the chow hall and get a lunch of their choice. This they do, and when those plates are cleared and the table is returned to its pristine condition, untouched sandwiches still on plates before each

Marine, the congressional contingency makes its appearance. They are preceded by very large private security guards. There is a certain bravado evident in private security guards. Many of them are former military, some having served in Iraq during the invasion, now earning big bucks for a private firm. They seldom wear helmets and often tennis shoes, while the rest of us necessarily wear Kevlar helmets and steel-toed combat boots. The military does not provide security guards for visiting VIPs. Suffice it to say they provide a larger, overall security situation.

The senators, uninformed that there is a lovely buffet awaiting them in the private lunchroom, come in carrying trays of food they have gotten from the chow hall. It is probably much better public relations for the senators to move through the chow line in the big room. At their tables, the senators begin by asking names and hometowns of the Marines seated around them and are soon in animated conversations about everything from athletic teams to family situations. Not much food is consumed. The senators distribute phone cards liberally and obviously provide an enormous boost to the Marines' morale. Looking at them, I guess that probably only a third of the Marines are over 21. It is a wonderful public relations success, and, as the Marines say, a force multiplier. There are many photos taken by the Marine Public Affairs team. It is a prime photo op, and pictures of the senators with the Marines will appear in local newspapers throughout their home states. After about 30 minutes, the senators are whisked off for a briefing with Lieutenant General John F. Sattler.

While the debate continues in the U.S. Congress about assigning women to combat positions, the Marine women I interview who tell me they have been in combat situations all say they were "just doing my job." That their job is often something that could be defined as an "assignment in or near land combat units" (the Department of Defense regulation that exempts women from combat) is not a matter of concern to them. In fact, several of the Marines comment that requiring congressional oversight and approval of personnel changes that involve their assignment seems to be uninformed interference in conducting the war in Iraq.

When OIF-1 (Operation Iraqi Freedom-1) began in March 2003, LtCol Sarah Cope (then Major Cope) led 44 male Marines in an MP Security detail escorting the columns of support vehicles following the troops up to Baghdad. They were in full MOPP (Mission Oriented Protective Posture) gear during the mission, protecting them from potential chemical or biological attack. MOPP includes a protective overgarment, mask, gloves, and footwear covers. The overgarment is impregnated with charcoal and acts to filter toxins and contaminants in much the same way as a gas mask respirator filter. With the weather variables pretty phenomenal (during the invasion, up to 90°F or better in the sun; 30°F or less in the desert nights), MOPP gear causes tremendous body heat buildup, which can lead, at times, to heat exhaustion. The protective mask and hood degrade the ability to see, speak, and hear. The rubber gloves restrict air circulation and limit the sense of touch and the ability to perform tasks requiring delicate manipulation. All of these problems can reduce combat effectiveness, but are considered necessary until the possibility of nuclear, biological, or chemical warfare is eliminated. Cope and her Marine MPs wore MOPP for the first 30 days on the road. At that point it was determined there was no NBC (nuclear/biological/chemical) threat in Iraq.

Being a female officer in charge of 44 Marines over a 68-day period, on the move, sleeping on the ground, without latrines, or showers or hot meals, and having to carry all their own water, food, and supplies, is standard; having to lead them in combat would have been necessary if the convoy they were escorting was attacked. Luckily, it was not.

During the entire mission, Cope was in a combat situation. They were there to protect the supply line of trucks and troop carriers. The long supply line included the convoy in which Army Private Jessica Lynch was traveling, which came under fire and from which she was kidnapped. That was definitely a combat situation. As Cope says,

> This war has made it a little easier for people to accept females in war because this is the first time females have been involved in every aspect, whether it's our people living in Fallujah in the CMOC (Civil-Military Operations Center), a female driver delivering ammo to the front lines, or leading a convoy. None of that has ever happened before. I think the combat Marines realize we're not really that much of a distraction, and we can do whatever's needed.

SSgt Gianniana Pinedo, MP and FSF, tells about being approached at a checkpoint into the city by a Marine who asked her to accompany their team on patrol, to assist by doing much the same thing she was doing at the checkpoint, interacting with female Iraqis.

> That was a new experience for me. So I said, "Sure, I don't mind helping." He came directly to me, and I answered without it going up the chain of command. I know what I did, and they [the patrols in which she went along to assist] got squashed for a while, and I ended up telling my officer-in-charge, "I don't want you to say anything, but tomorrow I'm going to go on patrol because they need me to search houses. Sometimes they find women in there that may be suspicious and they want me to search them." That's helpful. That's what we do at the checkpoints. She was fine with that and she talked to RCT-1 (Regimental Combat Team). They were fine about it. But eventually one of the females talked to her master sergeant about what we were doing and he said, "Female Marines are not allowed to go out [in

combat situations]." It went up to the CO [Commanding Officer] and the CO put out an order saying we were not allowed to go on searches. So it got squashed there. I felt bad about it for a long time.

In other interviews, I am told about having to search areas surrounding a camp during a patrol.

There was a small village nearby, and we looked to see if we could find any weapons—we had to know if anybody could shoot at us. I mean, the road we're on is right here and their compounds are right there. They had the high ground. So you go through and you make sure there's nothing there, no weapons. If you find weapons, you catalog them, and if there are male Iraqis around we'd keep them all in an area cordoned off until we move on. It makes it less dangerous for our patrols.

Another Marine comments, "Combat is only dangerous if you get shot."

And another says, "If you're a mech [mechanic] you can get shot, too, sometimes just by crossing the road."

1stLt Alexandra Plucinski tells me,

In this deployment I've used a lot of skills I never thought I'd use. In Iraq, I'm in a minority, actually doing combat actions in a combat zone, in a noncombat MOS. I'm a combat commander. I have a platoon of Marines and we lead convoys into Fallujah and the areas surrounding the city. We take supplies, packs, personnel, any type of support that needs to go to the grunts. We started doing these convoys right to the edge of the city before Al Fajr. They still had mortar positions there and they still had rocket attacks, so it wasn't a very safe time.

Col Jenny Holbert fills me in on the name Al Fajr. Fajr (rhymes with Roger) was the Iraqi name for the Second Battle of Fallujah, in November 2004, when the Marines launched their offensive. The original name assigned by the military was Operation Phantom Fury, but the Iraqis did not think it resonated with the people. So the prime minister renamed it Al Fajr, meaning "New Dawn."

2ndLt Samantha Kronschnabel, a combat engineer, is platoon commander of Charlie Company, the only female in her unit. Her unit builds strong points consisting of vehicle control points, entry control points, housing for the Marines in the city, and preparations for survivability if they come under fire attack.

Sometimes we'd have tents, sometimes we'd put up C-huts, which are little barn-shaped buildings about 16 by 32 feet. [C-huts are four-sided, quickly constructed wood buildings that temporarily replace tent dwellings and are varnished to minimize the drying effects of the sun and make them less permeable during the rainy seasons.] We use sandbags and HESCO all around the perimeter. A seven-foot HESCO barrier will protect against 50-cal machine gun fire. Living in the city is a danger every day. Someone will fire at your convoy, or on the work site, because we're working outside. I've gotten into a couple of firefights. When we're in the city I carry an M16 and a 9mm.

There are a lot of AOs [Areas of Operation] in the city, with different units. They put out patrols and do security measures. We have contact with anybody in the city who's working there. I lived in a room with 32 other Marines, all guys. We had to make showers, sometimes a bucket with a wall to step behind. And heads [toilets] were wherever we could find a place to hide, or we'll dig a trench with our heavy equipment and then cover it up when we move to the next site.

Ordinarily, it does not occur to civilians back in the States to consider how much building goes on in a war—how much heavy equipment, ordinary picks and shovels, and nails, lumber, and pipe are needed to build housing for an army. The amount of war materiel needed to equip and support the military in Iraq is more than in any other war in history. War materiel runs the gamut from weapons and ammunition, food, water, tents, and all manner of vehicles, to portapotties, toilet paper, computers, medical supplies, paper, toothpaste, body bags, heavy construction equipment, paper clips, calculators, dental equipment, fire engines, bunk beds, hundreds of millions of feet of concertina wire, thousands of miles of cable, plumbing, explosives, furniture, uniforms, searchlights and flashlights, and trillions of parts and tools. Logistics experts talk about the impossibility of bringing back all that has been sent to Iraq. When the American military finally leaves Iraq, it will have to abandon much of the infrastructure that is necessary to fight the war.

The combat engineers build the infrastructure for the troops as well as destroy things. Kronschabel tells me,

I love building stuff and I love blowing stuff up. We build things—bridges, housing for people; we make places safer for them to live in, for example, in the cities. And we also do some demolition in the city as well. We're called on to blow caches of weapons, maybe some houses that aren't safe. We're all qualified to handle explosives. My corporals and sergeants go out there, doing the calculations. I do the calculations, too, and then go check it. I like being in charge. I think it's great. I'd much rather be in the city every day than back on base. I love it.

I feel like I'm making a difference. I like the feeling of a mission accomplished. Every day there's a different mission and at the end of the day I think, "Hey, my mission's accomplished. I got this thing built. And they're a lot safer, now, in the city."

That the whole of Iraq can be designated as a combat zone is obvious in talking to many Marines about the attacks they have witnessed on base. I also witness an attack at Camp Taqqadum when a rocket is fired into the base area.

I am in the chow hall at about 1830 with Capt Amy Malugani, Public Affairs officer for Camp Taqqadum, Lt O'Neal, Malugani's newly arrived replacement, and Maj Sabrina Hecht. We are having dessert, chatting about mundane things, when a thunderous explosion stuns us to silence. It sounds close. It is a sharp, piercing blast, and I instinctively realize what it is, although I have never heard a mortar or rocket hit. There is a moment of absolute silence throughout the 500 or so Marines at chow, and then all hell breaks loose. Half the Marines dive under tables while the other half run for the door. Everyone buses their own dishes at the chow hall, and Marines are dashing out carrying their dishes and dropping food everywhere. I ask Capt Malugani what to do.

"Get down," is the answer.

I find myself under the table, a paper bowl of chocolate ice cream still perfectly balanced in my hand. At 70, getting up and down off floors is not as easy as it used to be, but adrenalin does the trick, and I am down in a flash—one hand free. I have no recollection of getting down—or up.

We listen for more booms, but there are, thank God, none. I keep asking what to do next. There is a lot of confusion. Malugani says they will sound an all clear, which leads me to ask, "How do they know there won't be more?" There is no answer to that.

After three long minutes, long enough to stop shaking, we get up and decide to leave the chow hall and go to my tent to get my helmet and bulletproof vest. As soon as we walk out of the chow hall we can see ugly red flames and a roiling black cloud pulsing high—60 to 80 feet high, above the tent peaks. It is a shock. I realize I had grown lazily secure in the surroundings of the Marine bases. This jolts me into remembering that regardless of how professional, how everyday the situation seems, I am in a war zone. I am surprised at the intense anger this attack arouses in me. Maj Hecht is furious. She yells the usual Marine expletives. It is another situation where something has happened, and the Marines, our finest fighting men and women, can do absolutely nothing about it. There is no way to find the perpetrator. The frustration finds no outlet, other than cursing.

Capt Malugani is desperate to get to a phone to report in. This is Lt O'Neal's third day in country, so she is getting a baptism by fire. Inside my tent, the squad leader has all the women Marines berthed there in their armor and is telling them to stay put. They have all been in country only a few hours themselves. Later someone tells me that running outside is a dumb thing to do. Those running outside were going to their quarters to get their body armor or to report in to be accounted for. Outside there are no HESCOs or cement barriers to protect you. If the chow hall or a tent takes a direct hit, that is something else. But if it lands outside the chow hall, the HESCOs keep the shrapnel from flying into the hall.

When the anger subsides in the activity of donning armor, I wonder why I am suddenly so calm and decide it is because it seems impossible that it is happening. Malugani and Hecht are all business.

I grab my vest and helmet and struggle with the chin strap—a Marine steps up calmly to help me. I go out with Malugani and O'Neal and head to the captain's hooch, a wood structure about 50 feet away where four women officers live. As we cross the dusty, dirt lane between rows of tents, we can see the fire engines parked to our right, about 30 yards down. There are no more flames, only bright lights. We hustle into her building and Malugani puts on her armor and prepares to go off to her office to be sure all her Marines are accounted for. O'Neal and I sit in camp chairs, and the captain says, "You might as well watch a movie." She puts a DVD in the player and is gone. So O'Neal and I sit and watch *Mona Lisa Smile*.

I am numb. The situation I find myself in is completely surreal. The sirens and shouts and sounds of trucks outside the building nearly drown out the soundtrack of the film. Surely, I should be doing *something!* Thoughts of fire spreading in a flash through all the thousands of cloth tents that make up the base are quelled when I realize that the fire was completely contained by the time we had walked to my tent—about 75 yards from the chow hall. I know I am doing the best thing I can do—staying put so no one has to worry about me. But the anxiety is terrific.

The lieutenant is totally distracted and says, "I'm so worried about my Marines." Because she is newly arrived, they cannot reach her to report in and she cannot find them. Malugani will take the calls for her. They are still *her* Marines for a couple of days until she leaves and O'Neal takes over. I am dazed with how bizarre the situation is: I am in a war zone, there has been a rocket attack, no one knows if there will be more or where they will impact, I can hear the chaos building outside as Marines run to duty and vehicles speed by, and I am watching a movie.

Someone pounds on the door—it is the husband of one of the women who lives in the hut. He is desperate to find her. He goes off and about halfway through the movie, another of the roommates comes in, her armor on over her green sweats. She declares the emergency is over. O'Neal and I decide to go our own ways, and I go to my tent.

In my tent, the Marines are out of their armor and sweeping the floor, moving the bunks, dismantling a broken one, getting ready for the arrival of many more Marines coming in during the night. The Marine in the bunk across from me puts on her armor, carries her helmet, shoulders her M16, and goes off to chow. "They still have the chow hall open?" I ask. "Yes, ma'am, they'll keep the hall open late for everybody that ran out or missed it." It is amazing how everything is just about back to normal.

Capt Malugani comes by to check on me and says there were casualties, but no one was killed. Two of us in the tent decide to go to the head as "battle buddies"; when I come back I read a little in the dim light and finally put my flashlight down and go to sleep, about 2100. The adrenaline has worn off and I am exhausted. I have no trouble getting to sleep.

All through the night, flights land with Marine replacements. The Corps is in the middle of a RIP (Relief in Place)—replacements coming in from II-MEF (2nd Marine Expeditionary Force) as the I-MEF Marines prepare to go home. Every hour or so three or four get directed to our tent. They stumble in with all their gear—two sea bags each, a big jungle-green cammie backpack, a smaller pack, and their M16. Some of them have even more bags. Marines deploying overseas are allowed 400 pounds of baggage each, including their body weight. But they have to be able to carry most of it themselves. When one of the Marines already bedded down grumbles that there are too many coming in, the woman Marine dispatcher (recognizable by the green light on her lapel) who has escorted these new Marines to our tent snaps at her, asks her name, and tells her to keep her comments to herself, that they need to settle these Marines for the night. By now it is crowded, sea bags are everywhere; the tent supervisor tells me that it is a fire hazard and that there are more tents with room next to us. But it will have to get sorted out in the morning.

The pace of every day of my visit to Iraq matches that of the women I am interviewing: up at 0630, off to the shower trailer, to chow, a long day of walking the dry, brown dirt roads between nondescript brown adobe buildings and walls from office to office throughout the immense base camp to interview and photograph these extraordinary women, 30 minutes for lunch, another 40 minutes for dinner, and more talking or interviewing until time to sleep. I am not allowed to photograph anything on the base—not the chow hall, not the dusty streets, not the office exteriors where I meet Marines. My photos often have backgrounds that would be off limits were it not for the Marine in the photo blocking recognition of landmarks.

I have no time to write, but download my voice recorder and photos into my laptop after every couple of interviews. My camera, recorder, and computer are recharged every night in the Public Affairs Office. Since I am allowed to be with the Marines every waking moment, I pick up lots of conversation and insight into how these Marines think and what they are feeling about the war.

I get so familiar with the area of the camp where I am working that I am allowed to go by myself when I do not need an introduction for an interview. Always, when I walk through the base, Marines, guys and gals alike greet me—"Morning, ma'am" or "Afternoon, ma'am." When I am with Lt Gilbert, he invariably returns the greeting with "Oorah" at the beginning, as in "Oorah, gentlemen" or "Oorah, sir." Oorah is said in the same tone one would say hello. Oorah is tradition with Marines, the enthusiastic cry used in any spirited situation, and also much heard in ordinary conversation.

Sometimes my path goes through the surgical unit, and there I meet Capt Knoop, a Navy surgeon in the medical unit, who seems curious as to who I am and what I am doing there. We talk about our children and their interests, subjects very removed from the war zone we are standing in. The morning after the rocket attack, I meet Knoop on my way to the Public Affairs Office. I ask him if he treated the men injured last night. He says yes; he had been out jogging not too far away and so went right to the surgical unit. One Marine went right into surgery, and the others were treated for shrapnel. There were more than five, but he does not say how many. There were no amputations. The incoming was a 122mm Chinese rocket and was a dud, but hit the wood wall next to the HESCO and set fire to the hut, burning the interior. The firefighters had the fire out within minutes.

When I walk by the site later in the morning, a fire truck is there still, as workers tear away the flooring and walls. There is no smoldering, no smoke. None of the adjacent tents or buildings are affected. It just looked like they were demolishing a building. A smudged mattress lay out in the lane. I could see the six-foot shaft gouged out of the HESCO alongside the wall where the rocket hit.

The firefighters are civilian teams, on leave from their departments all over the United States, much admired by the Marines for their expertise and their instant response, saving many lives.

Capt Amy Alger tells me five Chinese rockets were shot into her compound about two days before I arrived. Two damaged some equipment, but no one was injured. One landed 25 feet away from where she was having a meeting with her entire staff.

> We didn't have a chance. It came in while we were in the tent, during my evening staff meeting. We heard the whistle of the first two rockets come in, but by the time the third one came in, and we hit the ground, it had already impacted. We discovered later that it didn't explode, but it wasn't a dud. It has a blast radius of 300 feet, but it didn't explode. This is not uncommon.
>
> The Navy ordnance disposal teams came in but didn't want to take it out that night, so we put a skeleton crew on because it was still unexploded ordnance. They came about six in the morning with a backhoe and did the extraction and took it away and disposed of it.

1stLt Tara Russell, a Huey pilot, says that her aircraft took a couple of rounds in the days leading up to the battle in Fallujah. Those incidents do not make the news so the insurgents do not have feedback as to their tactics.

The next day our squadron came down to support us during Fallujah, and they had two aircraft shot down. It all happened within ten minutes of each other. That hit the news in 20 minutes because we wanted to beat the insurgents. They would say, "We shot down the helicopters and we have the pilots." But the U.S. releases it and says, "Two aircraft were downed, but we have everybody and they're safe." That's much better for us.

Our ROE (Rules of Engagement) are that you have to know you are seeing the enemy to return fire. If you're escorting another aircraft and it's not really affecting you, you keep going. We escort combat aircraft when they go out on missions, usually during the daytime. We also do surveillance, watch a mission and report "Okay, we've got people in trouble over here, we need to go in." They'll give you a coordinate, who you're talking to, and then you go. Then you see whoever is needing your support at the time, and whatever is needed: if they're in contact with the insurgents, if they need you to do reconnaissance, or ID a target. Sometimes if they're taking fire from somebody on the ground and they can see the insurgents have run into a house, and are sure the enemy is in that house, they'll get permission from higher up to destroy it, and then they'll call us and we'll go. We don't do a lot of that around here because it's too difficult to identify the enemy.

Cpl Stephanie Ullman, the Female Search Force Marine who was tapped to meet her senator at lunch, feels that combat for females is not easily understood.

I am not going to lie. Not every female can handle a combat situation just like not every male is cut out to be a Marine. You truly have to be dedicated to your job and understand that everything you do has consequences. All of your actions have an effect on someone. It is all about discipline inside and out.

If they did decide that females are not allowed in combat, then that would basically eliminate the entire FSF. This would open up another threat—of Iraqi women insurgents who could come and go without being searched.

Ullman's fellow FSF Marine, Sgt Lori Luna, tells me she reads articles talking about banning females from being in Iraq at all, due to the danger of combat. She says, "Do they realize what a difference these women are making in the war? What a big part female Marines have in influencing the Iraqi culture? It made me upset to read this."

LCpl Alicia Waters, also FSF, says,

The discussions about limiting women in combat frustrate me no end. All I want to do is to be able to do the job I am trained to do with no restrictions. Being in the military police makes that kind of hard. MPs get assigned to things involving the infantry and other places where females are not supposed to be. I am not asking to be an Infantryman. But I think the FSF program would be affected.

When the convoy carrying Searchers—their replacements that these Marines trained—is hit by a suicide bomber just four months after my interview with them in Iraq, these FSF Marines and I are in touch and we exchange e-mails about the tragedy. Some of them feel that tragedy could have been avoided if the women had been allowed to stay in the city rather than traveling back to base every evening. But that would have meant assigning them to billets in a combat zone—something that is not allowed.

1stLt Anna Reves is a platoon commander who worked at the edge of the city of Fallujah prior to the battle in November 2004, securing a large factory area on the main road. She also led the unit that recovered bodies of the enemy in Fallujah. Article 15 of the 1st Geneva Convention requires armies who bury enemy dead to record the number and names of the dead and publish or deliver that information to the enemy. "Enemy," in the case of Iraq, is misleading. The enemy is not Iraqi civilians, but insurgents, and telling them apart is not always easy. According to Reves, what they found on the bodies they recovered from the battle left no doubt.

"We don't do body counts," according to General Tommy Franks. His comment referenced the U.S. policy not to estimate the number of Iraqi civilian deaths caused by the Iraqi war, and it fueled the hue and cry from the antiwar groups in the United States about the toll of the war on ordinary Iraqi civilians. The U.S. government maintains that it is impossible to obtain an accurate count due to many factors, including the inability to know if the casualties are caused by American forces or the insurgents. There is also the fact that many bodies are taken up by families for immediate burial. In Islam, the utmost care must be taken of the dead, and they must be handled with respect and buried as soon as possible, so in cases of innocent civilian deaths, families often remove bodies before a count can be made. Bodies of insurgents were usually unclaimed.

I meet Reves at the Public Affairs Office, and we take chairs out onto the roof of a section of the building that sits next to the old control tower at Taqqadum airfield. It is late, nearing 2030, and Reves has not been to chow yet. We are able to take advantage of a cool breeze, but unable to get away from the roar of the generators alongside the building. I sit only 12 inches from the lieutenant and have to strain to hear her answers to my questions. She is slight, with large brown eyes and auburn hair just to the top of her cheeks. She has a composed, sensitive bearing. She is quiet and purposeful, and I wonder if it is the content of her story that makes me sense a haunted look in her face. "My team was tasked with recovering Iraqi dead in the city," Reves tells me.

> In preparation, we had to build a strongpoint: bunkers, posts at the entrance, and then it was a matter of standing watch, walking around the other Marine posts to make sure they're awake. We used passwords then. There was some activity while we were there, a rocket attack, and a sniper on the rooftop.

Once we took the patrol out to pick up a prisoner who had put out a bunch of trip wires for explosives. We didn't get too close. Somebody was usually out there with a mortar trying to hit us a lot of the time. You just had to stay alert. It got pretty cold while we were out there. It was okay if you were walking around or climbing the watchtowers, but if you were just sitting there for 12 hours, you'd get cold real fast. We had every warm layer on, rain jacket, and Gore-Tex. Then the day the battle started we had rain, typical Marine battle conditions.

We were back and forth to TQ and ran convoys. We had showers in TQ and sturdy tents. When we'd take a convoy into the city, we were provided with convoy security since we didn't have any with us. We had to block traffic and use pyro [flares] to stop traffic if we were making a turn onto a road or to stop traffic going the other way. If they didn't yield to that and got within 100 meters, then we start to use firearms and 16mm. Once we did have someone come up real fast on us and we had to fire on them. Then we had to block off all the rest of the traffic to walk out there and have a look to see if they were okay or were insurgents, whatever.

I have 40 Marines in my platoon, all men, and they're big guys. I guess I really don't think about leading them in combat. We're not infantry. We're taking convoys of supplies. Just last week, one night we were going down the main highway, the one we go down every time we go out. We have to go down that road no matter where we're going. There were about four or five [insurgent] firing positions one or two kilometers out that started to fire on us, the same place where we had taken fire the day before. So I called in to report that we were under attack. We have a computer system [in the Humvee] with a map that gives coordinates where we are. My Marines used their guns to return fire and no vehicles went down. Some of the trucks in the convoy had some impact but everybody was okay. We got through to our destination and checked all our vehicles. It's hard to know if we hit any of the enemy. Of course, we were aiming in the dark, so all we could see were muzzle flashes. My gunner, looking through his normal sight, didn't see any heat signatures from bodies; the only signatures he saw were from the muzzle flashes. They were probably dug in.

We sent a patrol out the next day, but they didn't find anything, no trails. If they hadn't been dug in, we would have done some serious damage. Each time we go out I look at the intel report to try to figure out what's going on, what's the latest tactic. Sometimes they have a decoy IED to stop the convoy and then have the real one go off, things like that.

I knew it was possible to be in combat, but that's the really great thing about the Marine Corps. All your officers, regardless of whether you're a supply officer or public affairs, all go through the same six-month long infantry officer training. You learn how to call in artillery fire, air support, you learn how to fire all the weapons, use grenades, and you go out there, back up in the hills, and practice tactical warfare. We did urban training before we left, but didn't think we'd use it. But then when we went into the city, we were operating in a combat environment. Because my Marines were driving on the convoy they probably never would have thought of urban combat. If I hadn't had the training I had, I probably wouldn't have been able to set up the secure perimeter at the strongpoint.

When we did the body recovery, we wore masks and gloves and recovered every possible remain we could identify as human. Things as small as thumbnails, toes, and other body pieces, often arms and legs, and even bones of bodies lying in heaps of bloody clothes that had been eaten by packs of dogs and feral cats. Sometimes the bones had been picked clean and were scattered so that we couldn't be sure we had them all. In the case of explosions, there were body parts everywhere, and we couldn't tell what parts went to which bodies. We picked up decapitated heads without being able to find a body to match them to.

We had to search the bodies for identification—go through pockets and look in shoes, wherever. That was the worst part, because some of the bodies were pretty decomposed or torn apart—sometimes disemboweled. In most cases, there was no personal identification on the bodies, although we did recover thousands and thousands of American dollars from pockets of the males. We were pretty sure ordinary Iraqi civilians wouldn't have access to large sums of American dollars. It was our feeling that the lack of ID pretty much indicated that the body was that of an insurgent, and not necessarily an Iraqi. There was no way to identify a body by nationality.

The extended battle was going on there, and we had to test the bodies first, for IEDs, before we could move them. We had a very specific setup team. We had a grappler we attached to the bodies and then everybody would get behind a wall out of the way and we'd yell "pulling!" and we'd make sure everybody was clear and we'd pull away the bodies. There were a lot of parts, like legs and torsos, sometimes dead animals who had been killed setting off IEDs in the bodies. And IEDs were found in dead animals, too. We put the bodies in body bags and loaded them in the back of a truck. Once we'd finished with the bodies, we'd go over information as to so many RPGs, rockets, IEDs, grenades, how they were killed, then we'd take the bodies back and Mortuary Affairs would process them.

We found things like cell phones with telephone numbers that were useful to intel, and paperwork that had directions on how to get into the country from Jordan, or Syria, where to go, who to meet with, where to get fake IDs, stuff like that. We got a lot of stuff on the bodies as far as addresses. A lot of the time bodies had weapons on them. We'd have to get everything off the bodies. Usually we had Marines who would throw the weapons over a wall to get them out of the way [insurgent weapons—later destroyed]. We found AK-47s, stuff like that. Those would all be destroyed.

The remains were put into body bags and taken to a military morgue to be registered according to the regulations of the Geneva Convention. If there was identification, or personal effects, such as a shirt, or cap, or some identifiable clothing, it was placed in a plastic bag and attached to the body bag, to be logged in and archived separately after the body was buried. Our team was out there for about four weeks. We would have three days in the city and then two days back at camp.

After the Battle of Al Fajr, records made available to the Iraqi Government list some 1,400 dead Arab males, 12 women, and 2 children. Prior to the battle, most of the original population of approximately 285,000 left the city. The Marines acknowledge that the insurgent leadership most probably all decamped as well, as is evidenced by the sudden increase of activity near Mosul and Samarra while Fallujah was under threat.

"It was impossible to know if the bodies we were recovering were good guys or bad guys," Reves continues. "We will never know." The Marine information on the population remaining in the city when they commenced the attack in November 2004 was approximately 15,000 people. Many Marines were quoted as saying Fallujah was a ghost town by the time they went in, and the ghosts were all aiming at them.

Reves describes the follow-up to their retrieval of Iraqi dead.

> Each body was logged into a database with coordinates as to where it was found and the type of wounds or cause of death, if known, or recognizable. Personal effects were also noted in the record, and these were archived separately for future reference, so that Iraqi families could make use of the data to look for family members missing in the city.

The bodies were buried in long trenches, with 18 inches of soil between each body bag, and with the bodies, as far as could be determined, on their sides facing Mecca, according to Sharia law. When the earth was replaced over the bodies, a Muslim military chaplain recited the prayers for the dead. The burial place of each body was marked by a metal stake on which is a number corresponding to the identification number for that body in the database.

Col Holbert explained that when the U.S. military began burial of the unclaimed dead, because nationality or tribal affiliation was unknown, it was decided to bury them according to Muslim tradition. An Iraqi imam volunteered to observe the burial process to give approval to the military. He also had no idea if the bodies were those of Arabs or Iraqis, Sunnis or Shia, but he observed the procedure the first few times and then gave his approval, saying he trusted the military burials to continue because of the respect shown for the dead. It was a sign of acceptance—a "good to go" blessing by the imam.

"We were very proud of the work we did," Reves tells me. "We handled the remains with the utmost respect and kept in mind that they were human beings, just as we are. I don't know of any case where any enemy of ours has done as much for our dead soldiers."

When I sit back and turn off my tape recorder, it is very dark. The moon casts pale gray light on the long, dusty runways and the sea of tents behind us. It is momentarily, deceivingly quiet—no flights going off, only the constant drone of the generators. Sitting so close to Lt Reves, I see the fatigue showing in her face. "I can't imagine a more terrible job than that," I tell her.

"No—my job wasn't the worst," she answers. "The worst job was the unit that had to collect the Marine bodies in Fallujah."

7

GUNG HO—FOCUS ON THE MISSION

Gung Ho—from the Chinese *gong he,* means working together. Actually, *ho* means peace or harmony, *he* means together. Gung Ho—work in harmony, gung he—work together. That is close enough. How did the Marines pick up the phrase? It comes from LtCol Evans Carlson USMC, of Carlson's Raiders, serving in China in 1941. Carlson was impressed by the Communist 8th Route Army that indoctrinated its troops in ways somewhat similar to Marine training. This was before 1949 when China became a communist country under Mao Zedong. During World War II in Asia, the communists were the only Chinese troops actually doing battle with the Japanese, and they were considered allies for a time.

Gung Ho is more of a battle cry these days and is used to indicate how tough Marines are, how dedicated to their mission. It is about pride.

"As a Marine, it's critical to have pride—in yourself, your unit, your team," explains Col Jenny Holbert.

> You have to know your job is important. Marines have to work well in a team. Each Marine has to do his or her part, and you have to be able to depend on each other. Every Marine, if they are a cook or an intelligence analyst, has input to the greater whole as part of the team. It takes a lot to make a Marine and there's no room for slackers. You're done in four years, if you don't want to make it a career, but you can't quit when you want—you can't move job to job, as in civilian life.

I found this a good way to describe the way women Marines feel about their training and their place in the Corps.

1stLt Blanca Binstock, a public affairs officer, is assigned to the Combat Operations Center (COC). The COC has a representative from every section, including staff, administration, legal, public affairs, logistic, etc. She will be the watch officer, with 12-hour shifts.

> Everybody needs to be aware of what's happening, whatever's going on in the field. Twelve hours here is a lot different than 12 hours at home. And

that's a good thing. At home, you have civilian dress, you have a car, you have to plan to leave early to drive to work. Here, you never worry about what you're going to wear and you just get up and walk to work. There are different stresses here. At home when you're off duty, you can read, go to a movie, eat out at a restaurant, surf the Internet, shop. Here 12 hours of work makes an entire day. The 12 hours you have off means laundry and other chores. But I'll get some time to read.

I like to read books about the Marine Corps. I know it sounds corny. I like first-hand accounts of what Marines have gone through. I think it helps me appreciate that no matter what happens, somebody's been through a lot worse and they've survived. People tell me, "It was different back then. It was a different war." I like to read about that. Like now, I'm living in a tent. I may not have hot water. I may not have water at all. No matter what, someone has always had it worse. I'm excited to be here.

Cpl Terianne Anderson keeps the logbooks for aircraft maintenance.

The things we do would probably seem ordinary. But everybody's proud of their work here. Sometimes, I'll be up in the office, and the alarm will go off that the pilots are coming in for refueling. They have only about 10 or 20 minutes each on the ground before they have to take off again. Everybody's working together to get the aircraft off. It's awesome.

Pride in being a Marine, to 1stSgt Connie Arline, means helping young Marines stationed in Iraq in administrative roles.

A lot of our Marines don't get out of camp. They are logisticians, comptrollers, public affair officers, and disbursers, all supporting the Marines. I'm in a position now, as senior enlisted advisor to the commanding officer in our company, to effect change. I like to get out and about and talk to Marines, see what they're doing, talk to them about their families, try to make things a little better for them. Some of them have concerns about being here. And it's a funny thing—they'll talk to me about it, but I don't know that they'd talk to another man. I'll just be out anywhere, "Hey, how are you? How's the wife? What's going on?" and then they'll start. "I'm having this problem—my wife—my kids." It's very difficult for them to leave all that and come here to a very different structure.

We have a company of Marines—about 230, throughout the area, and I try to get to the chow hall to talk to them, just so they know someone cares about them, and if they have a problem, or a family situation—well, I've been a chaplain, I've been mother, I've been all of these things to these Marines. Sometimes they just need to be able to let it out, to have a release, when they're going through these issues. Bring them in, talk to them. I like to see what I can do about their living conditions, get them calling cards so they can call home. Sometimes it's just being able to hand them something. Some of the ones who have performed well, I try to afford them the opportunity to go out on the humanitarian missions in the city of Fallujah.

Morale is good. It's about pride, and caring. It matters to keep the organization structured, moving along well, keeping the Marines motivated. That's what gives me joy.

1stSgt Laura Brown talks to me about mail.

It's mountainous, the mail that we get. If you were to see some of the mail containers, they're just humongous. It's nice to know that America doesn't forget about you. You can imagine, there are so many Marines out here, and you'd be amazed at the love that America shows us, all the packages and letters that come in.

The mail comes by air from the United States on C-130s flown by DHL on a private contract. It goes to hubs in Kuwait and Bahrain and then is sorted and the mail to deployed troops in Iraq is flown up to air bases in Iraq on smaller planes. The mail containers are off-loaded by Rough Terrain Container Handlers or RTCHs, called ratches. Brown is right, the amount of mail is enormous. In the first year of the Iraq War in 2003, 65 million pounds of mail were dispatched to the troops in Iraq, at a cost of $150 million to get it there. At that time, there were no postal stations and handlers, not to mention the big forklift equipment, to handle the mail. The military had to break down the containers and sort all the mail by hand. In just the month of April 2003, during the initial stages of the war, 11 million pounds of mail went to Iraq—almost 38,000 pounds a day. According to the U.S. Postal Service, that is equal to forty 40-foot trailers. The military was still engaged in fighting its way up to Baghdad at that time, so mail delivery was not the highest priority. All the trailers going into Iraq were loaded with ammunition, food, and water, not mail. Now, the current wartime standard of mail delivery within a 12- to 18-day period is being met.

My Marines sort all this mail. Civilians punch a clock, from this time to that time. Then they go home. As a Marine, you don't get to do that. When the mail comes in, you'd better be working the mail, morning, noon, or night, because you know somebody on the front lines is waiting for that mail. That's the price.

The Marines—the MPs—take it on convoys to the various camps. There are convoys going out almost every night. But if a place is hot, if there's an operation going on, then you can't deliver the mail; it's got to sit. But whenever the mail comes in, they try to hurry up and get it out. There can be mechanical problems. Once we had a plane that was too big. Or we didn't have a ratch big enough to off-load the containers.

My job is to make sure everybody has a clear head and can deal with these problems, and we're all on the same track.

Brown is looking at picking up the rank of sergeant major. She will know in six months.

I've told myself since 1985 that that's what I was staying in for. The dream is about to become a reality, I hope. When I'd been in the Marine Corps six months I knew that I was going to be here for 20 years, because I'd found myself. When you're somebody who has a type A personality, it comes easy to you. Being authoritative comes easy to me. And really, I'm a mentor. I'm not sure when I realized that; I just like to help people. When you know that you have those qualities, what better place to be than here? I've always known. That's what I've aspired to. That's what I've worked towards. I always knew what I wanted.

We probably have 500 sergeants major in the Corps. [There are about 160,000 enlisted Marines and 19,000 officers in the Marine Corps. Sergeant major is the highest rank among enlisted Marines.] Of those 500, there are maybe 10 that are women. The tunnel—it gets smaller and smaller. When I picked up first sergeant, there were probably 1,500 of us vying for 200 slots. So it's hard. It's very competitive.

I understand why I'm here in Iraq. I'm here for the Marines. I have to say, when I got here the first time, it was unnerving, because we all had gas masks and MOPP gear. That was scary, because you never know what might come in. The unknown is terrifying, overwhelming. There was camaraderie that came out of that. I'd hear people that were my daughter's age saying to me, "We're going to be okay, aren't we, First Sergeant?" And I'd say, "Of course we are." And then you'd look up to the heavens and say, "Please let us be okay." That's who I am. When you've been in the Marine Corps 18 years, it's not because I'm so wonderful. It really is because I'm continuity. I'm the calm in the storm. That's what the Marine Corps expects me to do. It's not because I do such a special job. It's about the calm I bring.

LCpl Jessica Kane, a radio operator who is the driver for her company commander, often drives him outside the wire to the city of Fallujah and surrounding areas. She draws her gung ho experiences from the pride she feels in the change the war has brought about for the Iraqi people.

In the overall picture, I think it's great what we're doing here in Iraq. Before we got over here, I didn't understand it at all. I didn't know about the politics of the war and the problems, the specifics of the everyday things. The only thing I know now is what I see over here. Like taking food out to a starving family in the middle of the countryside. And school supplies. It was a monumental experience to see these people who have nothing; they don't even have shoes on their feet. The Coalition forces brought them food and water and now the people have shelters and wheelbarrows and they have Iraqi National Guard soldiers watching out for them.

The look on their faces is different—it's a look of hope, almost, that they're building something, that they have a chance, whereas under Saddam they had no chance to better themselves. Some of these people never had anything. They didn't have safe water. Now they have water and electricity, and people seem generally to be happy. And that's great that we contributed to that.

LtCol Cindy Atkins, who, as administrative executive, tracks the whereabouts of Marines, tells her staff that personnel accountability and casualty reports are their main focus.

We track all the casualties and process the wounded, but I also get to forward the awards system. So I see all these maimed and mangled Marines and sailors, and then I read the award write-up on what some of them did. It's just heartwarming to know that these young boys—that's what they are, they're between the ages of 18 and 25—did such heroic things to help do the right thing for these people. It's something we take for granted. It's so the Iraqis can walk safely down the street, so little girls can go to school and not worry about being shot at. We cleaned up Fallujah and all of a sudden the next day we're helping them hold elections. The responsibility is phenomenal. And this is America's youth. That's how I look at it. The moms and dads of the world gave me their sons and daughters, and I want to make sure I give them back to them as safely as I can.

LCpl Mary Heathcoat, a radio operator who also works in patient tracking, finds her job very rewarding. She records the necessary data: name, rank, serial number, etc., for the surgical shop and trauma unit.

I had the opportunity, while I was talking with the Marines, to cheer them a little. They were hurting, and they liked seeing a smiling face, someone there to talk to and hold their hand. I kept track of their gear, too, and inventoried it. If they happen to leave without their gear, I contact their units and make sure everything gets to them, and nothing is missing. They can't keep track. They're hurting and they're rushed; they often leave their wallets and stuff. I reassure them when they worry about their things going with them, or wallets left behind that they'll never see again. I make sure it all catches up with them.

Two weeks ago I was still trying to get someone in a unit to come pick up the effects of a patient who died of head trauma weeks ago. But they've always been too busy. We had the Marine's wedding ring, and his wallet, and other things. Finally they came and then had to write a letter to the family saying why these things were so late getting home to them. That's such a sad situation.

All the information is put in the computer so they can access it from wherever the patients get sent. We track patients by number, and when they come in, we write the number on their body. Sometimes patients are intubated or in a coma, and we can't get much information beyond what's on their dog tags. We don't like it that they become just a number when they come in. I feel better that I can track them by name, because I had to record their name. I always remember them by name and call them by name. Yesterday, one of the new corpsmen [who doubted her ability to recall names] asked me if I could name five people off the top of my head who had been through there, and I named five people from before the corpsman was assigned because I could remember them. He said I was the first person he knew who could do that.

I was also in charge of giving the patients cammies or socks, shoes—whatever they need. I provided all that for them. It made me feel good, needed.

Col Jenny Holbert reminds me that these stories, coming out of a war zone, are the same for male and female Marines.

You could find a journal of experiences in Iraq and change "Mary" to "Michael" and it would be the same. All except for the combat stories. We are all sisters—and sisters to our brothers in the Corps. Despite personality differences and everyday attitude clashes, every Marine will defend their fellow Marines to the death. It's sort of a "don't mess with my sister" or "don't mess with my brother" attitude that transcends everything.

SgtMaj Suzanne How is convinced that her career is exactly where she should be.

It's the perfect place. I've devoted my life to it. I believe in it. I believe that with the certainty that I believe my religious convictions.

With pretty rare exception in my career, I was the only female or I was the most senior female. From the day I came in, I was always pretty much alone. I focus on my Marines. I tell myself every day when I wake up, the only reason I'm here, there's only one, is because I have Marines. If I didn't have Marines, there's no need for a sergeant major. If I don't have a commander, there's no need for a sergeant major. My world is my Marines. I've been married twice. I've divorced. My mother was disappointed that I won't have children. Finally, one day I said, "Mom, I've got 400 children. I've got 700 children. I've got 1,200 children." Then she got it. "All right," she said. I've got all the children I need. My Marines know I don't baby them. And that's why I'm here.

I was here during the war in 2003. It was great because all the Marines came together and nobody complained, and they all made good decisions and they were motivated—even though conditions were tough. There were 143 of us, only one other female, a driver. We were getting maybe a liter and a half of water a day and it was hot—in the 90s and 100s. It went on for two and a half or three weeks. Nobody took showers, we slept in the dirt, but it was great. When there's a war and you're in a fight, that's all you know. With all the stuff that's going on around you, sleeping in the dirt is nothing. It brought out the best of the Marines. They were in short supply of everything, like cigarettes, chewing tobacco, water, food. Still the Marines took care of each other. They bonded. I didn't have to ask them to help out their buddies, it just happened. Sometimes I would really worry about one or two, because I thought they were going to fold when it got really stressful, but it didn't happen. I couldn't have been more proud.

Capt Jennifer Morris, who is a communications officer, was still in a Marine Corps school when the war started in 2003.

I was watching my friends go, and I felt like I was sitting on the bench. My family and friends couldn't understand why I wanted to be over here, but I wanted to be part of it. Eventually, I got my chance. I wanted to see what was happening here. I wanted to see if the war was a mistake, if the news was just totally negative or what.

I do think the news focuses on the negative. It's more entertaining. Who cares if a school gets built? I guess it's not a headline story. We females aren't just over here being secretaries, and the Marines are doing a lot of humanitarian work now, since the battle. Female Marines are doing just about everything now. I don't know what I expected when I came into the Marine Corps. I think I just wanted to be a Marine so bad it didn't matter what job I got. When I was still in college there were no women pilots, no combat engineers in the Corps. A number of MOSs have opened up in recent years, and now I have a whole lot of friends who are pilots. They fly Cobras. They go shoot things. They drop bombs. And combat engineers—they're out on the front lines. We're out here and we're doing it, and doing a good job. I've actually met some male Marine officers who prefer women because women are a bit more meticulous and more detail oriented. I think some men joined the Marine Corps to prove themselves just like we did. Maybe they look to their right and there's a woman there, and maybe that kind of takes them down a peg. Maybe it's an ego-buster. But the military broke all the race boundaries and gender boundaries. And it works. It's interesting.

1stLt Alexandra Plucinski, a logistics officer, says,

There's nothing as moving as seeing Marines do their job. You give them the basics and they take off and everyone's working together and they do their job. I have a great platoon, an outstanding platoon, a great group of Marines. After a mission, I tell them, "You guys did great! You really impressed me. Every single day we go out and you follow through."

Most of the time I'm hard-assed, just because the job needs it. But in terms of counseling, dealing with problems, issues, I think they're more likely to come to me with their problems, especially with their wives. "How do I deal with this? How do I talk to her about this? What's she thinking?" I try to help. It's just like having kids. They're all professional, but when it comes to their private life, they're like kids. We didn't even stand up together as a platoon until we got in country. We didn't have a lot of time to train as a team. A lot of these Marines were just out of school, so to see where we are compared to where we were when we got here, it's incredible. There are a lot of fresh faces, and fear; they're terrified of dying and leaving their families behind. They put all their tactics, techniques, and procedures they've been taught to use even when I'm not there. They'll be on convoy with someone else and I'll hear that someone returned fire, or there was an escalation of force, and they did their job. They're great. It's hard to describe. You just have to see it. They're really a good bunch.

How do you find words to describe them? They're so young—18, 19 years old. Since I'm older, and had experience before coming into the Corps, I have an idea what they need to succeed. I ask them what they're thinking they need. "What do you want to learn about? Do you want to buy a house? Go to college? Have a family? What do you need to know about?" We'll get the information for them and then get on them to make sure they follow through.

When I came into the company last May, and got the new unit, the brand new platoon, I didn't know anyone. How are you going to know you can rely on the Marines to the left and right if you don't know what's going on in their heads, if you don't know the training they've had? So we embarked on a training process, very regimented. "We're going to do a convoy mission, You've got to believe you can do it." When we got here, to the theater, I knew they had the basics. They asked great questions. We played a lot of war games before we left. We war game over here when the pace starts slowing down a bit. "Okay, here's the convoy scenario. The Humvee ahead gets hit. You see your friend's body lying 100 meters off and he's still breathing. Do you follow tactics and continue on or do you stop?" You have them go through the emotions in their heads so they can be able to actually do that. That's been a big thing. You envision your mission and you walk yourself through it. You walk through every tough scenario. That's how we train.

SSgt Pinedo thought it important to go active to be able to come to Iraq.

I actually was what they call Inactive Ready Reserve for a year and a half, two years almost. So I was not drilling like other Reserves one weekend a month. I volunteered to come in for this. My belief is that you're not a true Marine until you've been somewhere like this. That's why I came back. It's combat. It's not supposed to be, but it is.

Capt Jodie Sweezey, in Logistics, came back into the Corps

because we're at war, and sometimes it gets in your blood and you miss it and you want to be in the fight. I remember the day I got out and that first day was like walking into a brick wall. I tried so many things, all very different, even corporate America. A lot of Marines go on to be law enforcement or federal agents because there's a similarity to it. I think just being a Marine, having the training, the whole package, brings you back.

LtCol Sarah Cope says,

You just kind of adapt to this life. You ask what makes the Marines special, and I'd say that it's that we're one big family. It doesn't matter where you go. That's why it's hard to become a civilian. You become a civilian and you start working somewhere and you get the first "Hi, how are you." Then you're on your own. In the Marine Corps, although we may not always get along well, we always look out for each other. It doesn't matter if it's a new unit coming in, we take care of them. Period. Because they're Marines. I don't think you find that in a civilian job. There's more back-stabbing, more I-want-the-next-promotion type of thing. We do have peer competition going on, but we look out for each other. We're certainly not doing it for the money.

We have several Marines over here who left high-paying jobs to come back in the Corps. One of them is a sergeant, a millionaire, whose job is burning the waste from the portapotties. Another was an investment banker who is taking a leave of absence from his firm. And there's a lawyer. He makes a fraction of his civilian pay. It's pride. Pride, dedication, and challenge. We have the same core experiences: boot camp, OCS, whatever. I think it's sharing the hardship, knowing it's for a cause.

LtCol Lori Reynolds, who commands a communications battalion says,

There's no finer organization than the Marine Corps. It's a challenge. And to look back and be able to say "I was a Marine."

We installed this communications network. I was worried that when I came back in September and these Marines were just coming in country, that they wouldn't take ownership of it because they hadn't built it. But in their time here, they not only took care of it, but raised the standard even more. Now we're handing this over to II-MEF, the 8th Communications Battalion from the East Coast.

Back in the rear, these kids are faced with all the temptations that any 18-, 19-, 20-year-old kid is faced with. The cell phone bills, the cool wheels with the rims that spin backward and cost $2,500 that they can't afford, the alcohol, the women, the drugs. But it's amazing to see what they can accomplish when they get out here. Moving this big battalion around, getting back on ship or moving it up from Kuwait, was huge. We had 120 vehicles. The network is all across the Al Anbar province. It's spread all over the place. But we get here, and we started getting shot at real good, in March and April. It was very frustrating because you can't shoot back here. You just hope the grunts out there are taking care of business to protect you. These kids, in the rear [in the States], they were stepping over the line every so often, getting in trouble, but out here—it was a flawless deployment. And they do it while they're getting shot at with a smile on their faces. We had 74 kids out of the 470 Marines that we brought out here in the first half, 74 that rolled over and are still here. And what do we offer them? Not a lot, really. We've got a chow hall and a PX. It doesn't have anything to do with money. They're out here because they want to be. They're doing what they came to do.

Sometimes their background includes a lot of family abuse. These kids get married way too early and they don't know how to communicate with their spouse. They get children before they've grown up themselves. There's a lot of issues back there. Out here, it's just all about the mission, about being Marines.

Capt Amy Alger thinks that being a Marine demands a realistic outlook. She is immensely proud of the Marines in her company.

The conditions here in Iraq are not as harsh as they could be, as wars go, but here it's sustained and indirect fire and these are young kids. I can't say I was a big proponent of this younger generation because, having been at Parris Island and seeing them, in many instances, just quit and walk away [from boot camp], and that's okay. Their parents reinforce their actions by telling them there's no shame or negative stigma associated with quitting, but there has to be, somehow, a personal sense of failure. These kids who are here didn't quit. They stuck it out. They've done the job here, and they'll take that back with them and pass that on. It makes me very hopeful for the situation back home, and I needed to find that hope. I was getting kind of down on some of the younger kids today, I really was.

What I'm really hoping for is that they're going to take back the dedication that they came over here with, and also a spirit of self-sacrifice and service. I hope they'll take that back to their communities and show their peers what it's like to be a good citizen and how important a vote is. They see here first-hand how much a vote is worth and what it means to these people. I don't care what side of the political fence you're on, take a stand and make it mean something. I hope that goes back with them.

Maybe it's just a matter of pride on our part. I honestly think there's a lot of value to having the Marines anywhere in the world. We have a tendency to do a lot more with less. I've trained recruits and I've trained officers at OCS. So I'm proud to see the young people of today in the Marine Corps with the dedication, drive, and determination they have to accomplish their mission and carry on the history of the Corps. Of course, there are people who aren't cut out for military service, period. Some want to become Marines because they want the identity. They never belonged to anything in high school. It's changed. Our bread and butter used to be the captain of the football team, the basketball team, the guy who was out hunting and fishing. That's not the case anymore. The paradigm has shifted. They [today's recruits] may just watch MTV and never really get involved in high school. But they want to be somebody. They want identity at least. That's what attracts them to the Marine Corps. The challenge is, how do you motivate someone who's never participated in a team? That's fundamental. You have to be a member of the team. You cannot be an individual. How can you motivate someone who's never been out of their comfort zone, doesn't play sports, and basically has never pushed their limits either mentally or physically? How do you keep them focused in training so they can graduate? With these challenges, based on how many of the young people we attract are raised and what they're exposed to growing up, this war is going to be a payoff. It's real-world. You can really see how, when it gets really tough, the cream rises to the top. I haven't had a single one of my Marines in this company that had to see the battalion commander or that got in trouble and had nonjudicial punishment, not a single one. Not a single one. I'm very proud of that. We accomplished our mission with 98 percent reliability across communication architecture.

That's phenomenal under these conditions. When you consider the extremes out here, the summers and winters, and the fact that this equipment has been continuously online for about 13 months—it was never designed to operate for that long a period under these conditions. It takes a lot of focus and attention to detail and making sure the equipment's maintained properly, that it's taken care of.

The problems in my field are because we have tactical equipment, like generators, but a lot of my servers, my laptops, these are Dell, commercial, off-the-shelf. We contract for it and we buy it, and then if we have support issues, we have to work through Dell and different companies to get parts and support. It's not like it was a couple of years back when everything was tactical gear—the computers were "ruggedized" tactical computers. Most of my gear is not. It's commercially available gear. It's tough to operate under these conditions, but it gives us more capability, and we need that capability because there are so many applications out here. The command requires so much bandwidth that we have to have the newest technologies.

We started integrating some of the gear. But, as with anything anywhere, you have integration issues. We could have certain things on a stand-alone network, and then there are certification issues and crypto [cryptograph] issues. Crypto is a whole other animal when you talk about communication architecture. It's been a learning experience just dealing with our supply system, getting parts for our tactical equipment, and also the tech support, the tech reps, just dealing with the new equipment. I've got Marines out here who had never handled it prior to coming out here. I have [computer] operators who have no experience whatsoever. They're just learning on the fly. I'm really proud of what we've done. There are so many "firsts" they've accomplished as communicators in this company with no prior experience.

For instance, fiber optic cable. We've put maybe 20 miles of fiber optic cable in the ground throughout the base. Commercial fiber optic cable, not just the tactical. We've probably run about 8 miles of tactical fiber. So just the technology out here alone, my Marines don't have any training on that. They've learned as they did it.

The challenges are terrific. Just for the cable—we couldn't get a contractor to come in here and make trenches for us, because the ground here in Iraq would break their equipment. So we're Marines—we're going to find a way, and if it means there's a Marine out there with a pick and shovel, then there's a Marine with a pick and a shovel. Someone to walk behind ditching machines and a small tractor ditch witch. We nursed those along and tried to keep them going. Pretty much at every turn there have been challenges, but all the obstacles and challenges have been overcome by their determination as Marines to succeed and to perpetuate the reputation of the company and the Marine Corps as a whole—because they're proud people.

They support each other. That's paramount. They take care of each other. They need to turn to each other for help here. We can monitor, we can try to provide the appropriate example, but everyone deals with the stress of being here. They deal with separation from their families. Some of them are married with very young children at home, the wife's pregnant, and so on. Everybody just has to deal with it in their own way and we have to figure out how best, as leaders, to be supportive and help figure out what works best for each Marine.

I'm responsible for the health, welfare, and safety of everyone in this company. If I failed in any one of those areas, I'd probably be out of a job, and I would deserve to be. I have a first sergeant and a terrific staff at all levels, and growing, so it's a team effort. It's all of us providing the right leadership and setting good examples. I'm proud of what we've accomplished. I tell my Marines that. I don't allow them to go [on missions] unless the mission dictates that it's necessary.

It's a little different for me. I don't have kids. I have a family, but I'm not responsible for anyone in my family. An extra consideration is that pretty much every one of us at some point in time has had a close personal loss over here, somebody that we knew well. Pretty much everybody I know has. I don't know how our country will react to seeing veterans without limbs, like after Vietnam. I'm serious. I get very emotional about it.

The following is a "farewell to the troops" written to the Marines of Capt Alger's company.

An open letter to the Marines of Communications Company

Marines, as we begin to pack our seabags and ALICE packs for our imminent return home there are a few lingering points I feel compelled to put to paper. While we came to this place as sons, daughters, brothers, sisters, spouses, and even parents, one fact remains above all—we came as Marines. We were more certain of our collective identity than any strategic, diplomatic, or tactical mission that awaited our arrival. We have endured, persevered, and even flourished under all too numerous challenging and dynamic circumstances and conditions. Your accomplishments are now a part of modern history made in a country that prefers to live in the past. Your untiring efforts have given the people of Iraq a future by paving the way for a fledgling democracy and opening doors to new personal freedoms an entire generation has never experienced. You are to be proud and commended for your accomplishments, for just as you have given Iraq a future, you too in many ways represent the future elsewhere. Institutionally you are the future of our fine fighting force and will be expected to perpetuate our reputation that has time and again been earned and paid for in blood. For those that chose to move on to civilian life you arguably have an even more vital role. I challenge you to rekindle in our society the spirit of sacrifice and service that you so selflessly demonstrated during your time in Iraq. Marines, you have a first hand appreciation that the right to vote not only holds tremendous significance in our governance but is also a responsibility incumbent on any good citizen and is a privilege not to be taken lightly. Chances are that while here you have been confronted with a close personal loss that has served as permanent reminder that freedom in fact is not free and many have paid the ultimate price so others might share in the same dreams far too many have taken for granted. With that thought in mind I'll leave you to consider the three legacies that are now entrusted to your care. First, you must perpetuate the legacy of our free and democratic society and be unyielding in the face of injustice and immorality. Second, you must pass these ideals on to your families and your children and raise them to strive to follow your example of dedication to duty by demonstrating an ethical character and commitment to our constitutional principles. Third, you are charged to always honor the memory of Marines like PFC Andrew Halverson, Sgt Rafael Peralta, Capt Alan Rowe and all other military members past and present that gave the last full measure to ensure our freedoms and safety. Marines, in closing, you are a unique dichotomy unlike any other. You have been faithful servants to the American people as well as sharp and powerful instruments wielded by our President in a time of national crisis. You have been perpetrators of violence and destruction and yet proved to be compassionate humanitarians. Above and beyond all else you are all heroes. Semper Fi, Marines, and thank you for a job well done!

Capt Amy B. Alger

8

THE FUTURE—CAREER MARINES OR MOVING ON

GySgt Amanda Vargas has five years until retirement from the Marine Corps. "I think I'll retire at 20 [years]. I want to be there for my son and my family. I want to buy one house. I'm tired of buying new curtains," she laughs.

All the little things in life, you know, every time you buy a house: new curtains, a new mop, a new broom. You make it your home, but you know it's temporary. With retirement, you can be home. My son will be 15 by that time, so he'll almost be old enough to be on his own. It'll be his last two years of high school. He doesn't live with me currently. He lives with his dad, my ex-husband, in Indiana. But at least he'll have somewhere he can come to always. It'll be his second home if he chooses to live with me. I think 20 will be my magic number. And I'll be young enough to start another career.

I plan to get my bachelor's degree at the very least before I get out. I want to be a teacher. I've always wanted to be a teacher, since I can remember. It's got to be something in education, either teaching or administration, because administration is something I've been doing for 15 years. I've learned to do it pretty well. Teaching is probably my passion. When I was a drill instructor, I really loved it. I loved teaching classes. I always volunteered for classes. I always liked doing that.

I love children. I love to work with kids. If I could, I'd probably open a business. That's another thing: the child care business. I've seen how hard it is for women who are single and don't have child care. And I would want to work with challenged kids. I would like to work with low-income families where I grew up, in the neighborhood where I grew up, the people that I know. I could show them that they don't have to settle for less.

A "19-year-old veteran" is the way LCpl Crystal Groves describes her status once she returns to the rear from deployment in Iraq.

I had a fiancé. I got my priorities straight once I got out here—you know, thinking about stuff all day long. Right now I don't want to concentrate on marriage or kids. I want to concentrate on education and saving money so I can have my family and support it when I get older. I explained that to my fiancé. He didn't want to believe me at first, but that's how it is.

He joined the Marines because of me. Well, not completely, but I had a big influence on him. He didn't have any plans after high school and neither did I. The applications for college, I felt like "Oh, no." But joining the Marines, I thought, *Come on, let's do it!* He left for boot camp about a month after me. He's back at Camp Pendleton. He was lucky, he got out of infantry school later so they didn't send him over here. I don't know if he thanks me for it or what. I still want to be friends with him, but I know it's hard sometimes. Believe it or not, there are a lot of divorces. I'd say six out of ten people get divorced. A lot of it is the separation. I know I had that problem at first, but then I started realizing what I really want: an education.

My mom raised me to be independent. I'm really proud of my parents. I know it sounds ridiculous, but my parents raised me exactly how I want to be. If I want to do something and you tell me I can't do it, if I really want to, I'm going to do it. And I will do it. A lot of that came from my mom and dad. That's not to say that they made the choice to enlist for me, but the important things in life, they taught me to concentrate on those. I'm 19 years old. I've got a whole life ahead of me. I'll get out. I'll get out of the Marine Corps two months after I turn 21.

As for 1stLt Alexandra Plucinski's future, she says,

I wish I had an answer. I love the Marine Corps. But I've had a lot of experience in the civilian world and in many cases, in my expectations, I've been tremendously disappointed. At the same time, and I know this is an issue for a lot of Marines, I can't have a family because with my marriage—he's locked in for ten years as a pilot. I'd love to stay a few more years, I know that for sure. So I'll extend. I'll probably make captain and after that get out and do something else.

There are a lot of things I want to do. I want to write. And I've always loved reading. I read mostly fiction. And I love reading about people's experiences traveling. If I weren't married, I would probably stay in and go on Marine Security Guard duty or work as a foreign officer in the State Department. I like security detail in the Marines. I like carrying a gun,

she laughs.

There are other factors. You could work for a security company at the UN, or the State Department, but could you protect yourself? I can. Or kidnapping. I have so many skills. That was one of the things I reassured my parents about. "I will be so well taken care of, and after the training I've received, I don't want to tell you how many ways they taught me to kill someone. I can take care of myself."

And deployment is tough on a marriage. If you're married to a military man, it helps, but regardless, deployment is a problem. You definitely have to be present to make a marriage work. It ultimately comes down to making choices. I'm almost 28. I know I still have a few more years before I start having a family. I want to enjoy my time now. A lot of Marines get married at 18 or 19. If I'd done that, I could have several kids by now.

I love what I do and I love being a Marine. I have never been so professionally challenged, and I love the daily pace. But there are callings for another life for me, mainly that of attempting to have a normal relationship without an interruption every six months. And eventually having a family. I never thought I would be a woman who would say that, but just as I felt the call to go into the Marine Corps, I feel the same call now to have a family in a civilian environment. Every Marine I know is convinced that I won't get out, but we'll see.

Capt Amy Alger comments,

Obviously, I will stay until 20, and it'll put me in an interesting bind, because at that point in time I'll be getting looked at for lieutenant colonel, so that's a carrot. I don't know that I can pass that up. I love it, and the realization is that in my professional life, this is all I know. This is all I'm really good at. But I don't know where my personal life will be at that point. I don't know if it's going to be the moment that I decide I just want to be in one place, that I would enjoy a desk job. I can't see myself giving it up right now, but I don't know. I really need to start thinking about that. It's not that far off.

Looks like I'm going back to Quantico to be on the instructor staff at Expeditionary Warfare School, so I can essentially retire from there. I've been selected for major, so I'll get promoted to major this September. I'll be heading back in three weeks. It's going to be bittersweet. Am I ready to leave? In many aspects I am, in many I'm not. I have command of circumstances in this environment; this is what I've trained for and I wouldn't want to be anywhere else. I waited 15 years for the opportunity to be in a situation like this, 15 years. I would stay, but there are other things I have to do in the Corps, so I'll have a go at it.

I'm going to miss it. I think oftentimes we discount our experiences. Certainly it's true that people don't understand about Marines—that we are very cosmopolitan. We're not dumb, knuckle-dragging Marines whose best talent is to be behind a rifle. There's so much more to any Marine, a lot more substance, a lot more character, and integrity. That's what neat about these kids. You see their character and integrity grow with experience out here.

A large component of the company will be going back to New York City, looking for jobs, going to school, recovering their lives, going back to whatever they did prior to this. They'll have a sense of accomplishment about being here; they'll be better people for it. They'll be better citizens. It's going to be an interesting transition for them. I'm counting on their taking these values with them.

LCpl Mary Heathcoat is not sure if she will stay in or not.

I think it depends on where I am. If I'm a corporal or sergeant I think I'll reenlist because it would be a good leadership experience. I haven't really had a chance to be in charge of more than one person, or an actual group of people. And I'd like the chance to use my initiative. I don't want to be an NCO that tells the troops what to do but then just sits and watches them. I want to be one of those that says, "Hey, we've got to do this." Make sure they do their jobs, but with my help. I think you get more respect if you actually help them. They're going to follow your example.

I didn't want to come out here with a boyfriend at home because it was too much aggravation. I didn't want to worry about what was going on back home and stuff like that. I want to get married eventually because I see how happy my mom and dad are, and I want to be happy like that. I have two years to decide.

LtCol Cindy Atkins will retire, again, from the Marines when she returns to the States.

I feel good that I was able to contribute here in Iraq. You can't stay in the Marine Corps forever. By law you have to go at a certain time. I wasn't at that point when I came back in to come over here, but now I've reached the point in my life when it's time to move on and make room for others to move up. But I'll miss it. You miss the Marines, because the Marines are so amazing. But everyone has to leave sooner or later, to move on.

When you deploy, in times of war, the bonding and common issues you deal with, the things you experience together, are different than life in the rear. I'm sure you heard about the rocket that hit back here a while ago—six or seven months, I think. It killed a major and badly injured a colonel, but he got fixed and he's back here. He went out to Germany and then to Bethesda, in Washington, D.C., and did rehab, and came back. He was the regimental commander. As Marines, we have these experiences in common, and it creates bonding. I hope it stays that way as we move on, because you need to keep that connection. There's a new call, for warrior transition, where everybody will stay in touch. That's what people need 30, 60, 120 days afterward—they need to be in touch wherever they are.

The Warrior Transition begins while Marines are still in theater, Col Jenny Holbert tells me. A two-hour session prepares Marines for what it will be like when they return home. The Warrior Transition program impresses upon them that it is good to tell their stories. It helps feelings come out, and Marines learn that dealing with their reactions to those feelings can sometimes dispel, sometimes exacerbate family issues. It is difficult, in some cases, to talk about Iraq to friends and family who are not as wrapped up in the war as those who have been there fighting it. It can lead to Post-Traumatic Stress Disorder (PTSD), which often is not evident until 30 days or more after a Marine returns from the war. Avoiding talking about experiences can lead to alienation, and eroding trust of people close to them and the world in general. There is sometimes an overwhelming feeling that people "just don't get it." It is suggested that Marines limit their time watching TV or violent movies, as often the emotional response to the violence witnessed in Iraq can be triggered by watching media coverage of the war. It takes time to come down from being deployed.

The leadership watches for changing behavior among Marines serving in Iraq and can recommend that a Marine be screened for PTSD if the situation warrants. Officers heading to the rear after deployment meet one-on-one with the chaplain. On returning home, Marines fill out a detailed, six-page health questionnaire. At 30, 60, and 90 days out, there is a folder of information to benchmark how Marines are doing as they fit into civilian life again.

LCpl Jessica Kane, whose legendary Thanksgiving letter home you can Google, thinks it will be a difficult transition to go home.

> It's going to be hard for all of us to go back. I'm working now on how I'm going to do that. It'll be great to get back. I'm excited about getting back and talking about it every day. It will definitely be a big transition to get back into that mode of life, because here we have a schedule, a plan, things we do every day. We're a well-oiled machine right now. It will definitely be strange to go back to lead a normal life. But I think a couple of weeks on the beach and we'll get right back into it.

Cpl Michelle Garza will be heading back to Camp Pendleton, California, and already has orders to Hawaii. "That was part of my reenlistment incentive," she says.

> My husband and I are going back home together.
>
> There's still more I want to do, a lot more. With my reenlistment, I'm obligated for another four years. And I think in another two I'll decide if I really want to stay in, or where I really want to be after these four years. I'm trying to finish school—get that out of the way. If I have enough school to support myself after the next four years, then I'll probably get out. That's my fallback. I think in two years I'll decide if I want to go on, go to the drill field—and I was actually thinking about putting in a package to go the officer route. It all depends on where I am at that time.
>
> I hope that in Hawaii I'll be able to put in more time to go to school—take classes at night. The Marines usually help you work your schedule around that. They understand that you're trying to get an education. I also want to have children. I was pregnant before I came out here, but in March I had a miscarriage. Otherwise I wouldn't be out here. I believe things happen for a reason, and maybe it wasn't right for me to have a child just yet. I'm still young. I'm only 22. So we'll see. I'm not sure I can plan, because with the Marine Corps, depending on what you want to do, you have to work around things. I don't want to be pregnant in Hawaii.

Cpl Brandie Collette, a field MP and combat vet, plans to finish college and become an art teacher. She has taken "a million pictures" of her experiences in the Marines.

1stSgt Laura Brown is looking to pick up sergeant major.

My husband is a first sergeant as well. About 15 days after I get back home, he'll deploy here for seven months. We have an 8-year-old daughter at home. She's with my parents in Washington, D.C. We've also got a 20-year-old who's attending North Carolina A&T (Agricultural & Technical State University). As long as you keep the allotment check going, she pretty much manages herself. We just shut down our household every time one of us has to leave. Right now the house is shut down. I hire a gardener who takes care of the lawn. My husband comes and checks on it every once in a while—he's stationed at another base. It's a hard life, but it's one that we choose, and we can't imagine anything else. I'll know about sergeant major in the fall. My dream is about to become reality, I hope.

1stSgt Connie Arline is ready to go home after six-months' duty at Camp Fallujah.

I think we've accomplished a lot since we've been here. I have not decided to retire yet. I'm really kind of playing it by ear right now. I can retire if I like, but it's very difficult to give it up. Just last weekend, for the first time in almost 21 years in the Marine Corps, I went on a convoy. I rode in a scout vehicle. I was just enamored and amazed at the job that the lance corporals did when I was in the vehicle. They were just very good. I was so motivated all over again. And I was thinking, it's very difficult to leave. I know one day I'm going to have to.

I could stay. I'm on the fence, actually, right now because of my daughter. She's 4 years old, and I've missed three birthdays and three Christmases. You can't ever go back and replace that with any amount of toys. So I'm on the fence right now. I'm holding on because this is 21 years of my life. And the camaraderie, it's awesome. I could be anywhere in the theater, as a Marine, and there's a courtesy that goes with that. So to lose that—it's going to be tough. But if I get out, I'm willing to go where the job is. I've moved around a lot, so it doesn't bother me to start again in another place.

SSgt Alison Arnold says,

I have two and a half years left. I'm over the hump. I'm halfway there. But it's so hard sometimes. There are times when I think *Okay, enough is enough.* I love the Marine Corps, but I want to raise my son. There are a lot of other single moms in the Marine Corps. We all feel guilty. We all carry this sense of guilt around for being out here, being away. It's difficult to make that choice. You want to be out here with your Marines, you want to be with your child. It's a constant battle. At home on the drill field, it was crazy. The hours out there are long and strenuous. When I went out [to instruct at the drill field] my son was 4. When I left, he was 7, and I missed all that time because I was working so much. I think that's been the hardest part of the deployment for me, being away—but even when you're stuck in the rear, you want to do your best on the job, so you put in all these hours, staying later than some of your counterparts. You want to do a good job, but you're torn. You want to be home with your child. I know I carry around a lot of guilt all the time. I'd feel guilty if I wasn't out here with my Marines. I want to be with my son. I feel guilty that I'm not with him. But it's worth it. It pays off. It's still worth it.

My son is 9, now. He's back in Camp Pendleton with his father. Emotionally it's hard, missing his birthday, missing the holidays. He thinks his mom is out here killing the bad guys,

she laughs.

When I call home, he's always asking—what's his phrase? "Did you get any action today?" And I'll tell him that no, I went to the chow hall, went to work, like any other day. Of course, everything's more dramatic for him. Actually, we have it relatively easier than our fellow Marines—the grunts— have had it. We don't have too much to worry about here on base, other than incoming and maybe bombs and stuff.

This is my second reenlistment. I remember going through the indecision about it, but it was in August 2003, with the war still going, and even though I was pretty set on getting out, I couldn't do it. So I signed on for another tour. Sometimes when I can step back and look at the whole thing I think there's still a lot that needs to be done over here. I don't think this is my last time over here. As for the politics back home, what it boils down to is, this is what I signed up to do. If I'm told that I need to come back over here, then I'm going to come over here and make the most of it, do what I'm paid to do.

1stLt Sara Hope has orders to Parris Island, South Carolina, as soon as she gets back.

My husband's already down there. I'll do my time at Parris Island, and then I have no idea what I'll do. I change my mind every day. Some days it gets kind of rough and I think, *All right, this is it. I'll do my tour and I'll be done.* But to be honest, working with my detachment made me think that the Reserves might be something I'd be interested in. I hadn't really thought about that before. Every once in a while the active duty guys come over here and speak about what the Reserves are like. My Reservists were unbelievable. I mean, incredible, incredible Marines. I gained a lot of respect for the whole organization working with them, so I think that's something I might think about doing as well.

1stLt Tara Russell comments,

I have six years left on my contract. It's six years after wings, and it took me two and a half years to get my wings, so then it's six years and then I'm going to get out. I've decided I won't stay.

I want to have a family. Who knows. When God sees fit, it will happen. I might go back to teaching. I'm a high school biology and chemistry teacher. That's my degree. I might be a guidance counselor. I have some interest in a charity project I'm thinking of. I'm not worried.

1stLt Anna Reves is up for a regular commission.

If they approve me, I'll probably go ahead and accept it. I'd have two more years after that and I could get out. So I'm probably going to go ahead for four more years. I think we made a contribution here in Iraq. For my Marines, it's a reason to give these people back their country; they're running convoys out here, getting shot at, all to help these people out. They have to be on the watch at all times. Along the way they've learned some Arabic, they got to work with Iraqi soldiers, and they got to see that Iraqi people have family, friends, and it's a very tribal world. Very old world culture. It's vastly different and a learning experience.

The Female Search Force group of Marines, after coming together in a unit that was the first of its kind, formed a special bond during that time, and each will go her separate way when the group returns home. LCpl Alicia Waters plans to take a couple of months to visit her mother and then go back on active duty in time to help with Toys for Tots. She will volunteer to return to Iraq when her unit deploys again in six months. "I am attached to the MP company in a Reserve unit and am not required to come back, because I've already done two tours. But I really want to come back. I'm 22, not married, and I do not have any children."

Toys for Tots is an annual program of the U.S. Marine Corps Reserves that gathers unwrapped, new toys for distribution to needy children at Christmas throughout the country to deliver a message of hope and inspire children to become good citizens.

Cpl Stephanie Ullman plans to reenlist. She will be stationed at Camp Lejeune and will return to Iraq in the next rotation, in August or September. She is 22, not married, and has no children.

Sgt Lori Luna will be reunited with her one-and-a-half-year-old daughter and will be discharged in August.

Cpl Becky Brooks plans to reenlist and will work at Lackland Air Force Base in Texas training military working dogs for the K9 Corps. She is 22, not married, and has no children.

Sgt Erin Black has seven years in the Corps and plans to make it her career. She is married. Her husband retired from the Corps the year before she joined. Her children are 3 and 5. She missed their birthdays while she was in Iraq. She will deploy again to Iraq in the coming year.

The world these Marines will soon leave is a no-nonsense realm with few amenities, and yet I never hear them yearning for the luxuries the rest of the world takes for granted. It is the people in their lives they want to get back to. Surrounded 24/7 with their fellow Marines, and totally focused on their mission, their entire world is in Iraq. Home is a dream, or a memory.

Home is also the origin of the hundreds of thousands of letters and banners and drawings that can be found in the hallways of buildings, on walls in offices, and in chow halls—wherever there is space. These are from schools and individuals from all over America—Hawaii to Maine.

They are from people, young and old, who have not forgotten that the Marines are away at war. There are more coming all the time. They are so heartwarming, and the Marines never fail to smile when they point them out to me—they mean a lot to Marines a long way from home.

What sort of a world is it that these Marines are leaving that they are loathe to leave, as much as they are anxious to go? In Camp Fallujah, I live in the officers' quarters that are located in solid buildings—adobe look-alikes. Rooms are Spartan, about 10 feet by 12 feet, with a bunk bed, a table, and a window. The women spruce them up in varying ways with trunks, canvas chairs, makeshift shelves, lamps, photos, pictures, fabric draped on the utilitarian room-darkening drapes. No one spends much time in their sleeping quarters, but it makes them nice to come home to after a long day, if they are personalized.

Bathrooms, with shower and toilet, are shared. The toilet cannot digest solid waste or much of anything, so there is a large covered trash basket for paper and all other but the stuff you simply have to flush. The floor and part of the walls are tiled in white, and the sink has small spaces that slope too much to keep anything laid on them from sliding into the basin. The Marines have put up a polite sign urging everyone to be conscious of the need to keep the space as clean and tidy as possible since it is a shared, uninviting space, and it is the best that can be expected. Hot water is limited. The pressure may be nonexistent, or sometimes drop to nothing mid-shower. The shower is a corner stall with about four inches of tile around the base and a curtain that does not reach all the way down, so the floor is constantly wet. Dressing without dropping your pant legs in the water is impossible. There is no bench to sit on or lay clothing or a towel. But it is private. One can shut and lock the door. Otherwise, there are no places where you are alone.

Portapotties also provide this privacy, but they are not a particularly savory place to spend much time, especially when the temperature climbs to the 90s. Enlisted Marines put on earphones and settle back on their bunks to write letters home, or read. They tune out the other 40 women who may occupy their tent, but they are never alone.

If schedule permits, the base library provides some quiet time. In Camp Taqqadum, the library is a converted Iraqi cement block building not far from the chow hall. It has multipaned windows set in metal frames and has two rooms of shelved books, each about 20 by 25 feet, with smaller study, or meeting rooms on each side of the main rooms. There are thousands of books, including dictionaries, Bibles, the Koran, thesauruses, a whole bound edition of the Harvard Review, books on Irish castles, English manor houses and gardens, Gibbon's *The Rise and Fall of the Roman Empire,* introductions to Farsi, French grammar, Arabic, and whole shelves of fiction: Dickens, Stephen King, Hemingway, Tolstoy, Diane

Mott Davidson, and a whole shelf of Danielle Steele. There is no Dewey decimal system or computer numbering here. The word FICTION is taped on some of the shelves, but you may find Stephen Hawking or T. E. Lawrence next to *Star Wars*. The foreign workers contracted by KBR to sit at the sign-in table do not, as a rule, speak English and therefore cannot use the English alphabet to arrange the numerous volumes—it is helter-skelter.

There is a wall rack of about 40 current magazines, all one month old. Stacks beneath hold back issues. *Oprah* is here, and *Vogue* and *Sports Illustrated, TIME, U.S. News, Reader's Digest*, as well as *People, Star*, and *Glamour*.

At the sign-in desk I am asked only to record my name and unit, the time I entered, but not, thank goodness, my blood type. I interview several Marines in the small rooms in the library and then photograph them outside, in the glaring sun. Alongside the library building is a series of dilapidated shops and a restaurant, now vacant. One closed and locked, glass-fronted shop has dozens of Iraqi pottery vases inside, all collecting dust. They are medium to large round shapes garishly painted and adorned with ripe clay blossoms draped around their necks. There are a few other knickknacks—a life-sized bust of Tutankhamen, for instance. The only shop that is open and doing a brisk business with Marines is a leather goods shop—shoulder holsters and knife sheaths—and odd CDs. At the end of this commercial area, a building has been remodeled into an Internet café. There are small, white Christmas lights framing the front windows so the building can be found 24 hours a day. Like other Internet cafés throughout the bases in Iraq, this is a plain room with perhaps 15 PCs for use at $1.50 for 30 minutes, $3 for 60 minutes. At the side is a long line of chairs with bored, sleepy Marines waiting their turn. One hour is the limit, because of the wait. If you have not finished the solitaire game or clicked on SEND at 60 minutes, your screen goes dead. As at the library, foreign contractors man the desk. They waggle their fingers at you when it is your turn and sign you in—and take your dollars when your time is up.

The bases are seas of blue plastic-covered tents as well as some hardened structures that are officers' hooches (hooch—a shanty-like dwelling, not to be confused with another definition of hooch—alcohol), and the command centers, and the chow hall. The tents are yellow canvas, manufactured in the Middle East, decorated inside with a band of floral designs at the top of the side walls. They rise to about 20 feet on tent poles mounted with long, vertical fluorescent lights. At the base of the pole is a fire extinguisher. The side walls are about 6 feet high, and the tents are lined with maroon metal bunk beds with curlicue metalwork in the head and footboards. Mattresses are covered in tough plastic with cardboard corners protecting the quilting.

There are few trees or shrubs to be seen. Concrete barriers, HESCO containers, sandbags, and portapotties are everywhere. The portapotties are along the roads and byways in lines of two, three, six, or eight, depending on the number of people living or working nearby. You find them along lonely roads, and in fields. You carry your own toilet paper always, because although contractors clean and service the heads regularly, the toilet paper supplies never last. At each group of portapotties is a wall-mounted dispenser of scented disinfectant gel that everyone uses liberally. Eventually, everyone exudes the same scent, sometimes oddly mixed with the smell of sweat.

I imagine a vast cargo ship passing through the Strait of Hormuz and slowly steaming across the Persian Gulf to Kuwait, full of hundreds of thousands of portapotties to be transported up to Iraq and placed in every conceivable space where they might be needed. And what will become of them when the troops come home? Iraq will inherit all these wonders of civilization, along with millions of other items—the detritus of war—some of it usable, some not. And who keeps track of where they all are? In Al Anbar, that is not the job of the Marines, many of whom are in charge of supplying the troops with everything else. Portapotties are part of the vast contract network that supplies the overall war.

I meet a cheerful middle-aged woman contractor named Ruthie, from Texas. She lives in one of the structures among the Marine tents and organizes the fun and games that are provided for the Marines. Her job is to provide whatever the Marines want for recreation, if she can. There is salsa dancing one night a week, and flag football tournaments, and chess matches. There are football parties to watch the games in the States, with the same snacks people at home will have. There is a cardio gym, an aerobic gym, a movie theater, a game room, and ping pong is available. Ruthie puts up flyers all over the base announcing what is going on. The recreational facilities are open 24 hours a day to accommodate differing duty schedules. Ruthie and her team of KBR contractors—Filipino, Pakistani, and Bosnians—work 12-hour schedules. Mostly, she says, she just hangs around and talks to the guys to provide cheer.

All of this is just diversion, the Marine women tell me, should you need it, from cramped living quarters, living out of seabags, having sand in your toes and in your clothes and in your weapon all the time, wearing 15 to 20 pounds of armor all day, walking everywhere, having the showers a lot farther away than you would like, not being able to brush your teeth without carrying a bottle of water along with your toothpaste, carrying all your personal gear into the showers and heads and having no place to put it down—all the minor details that you learn to live with.

No one thinks of it as hardship. It is what Marines do, and it is a whole hell of a lot better than being outside the wire where there are no amenities at all. After six months to a year, it wears you down, but by then you have forgotten it was ever any other way.

The scent of cigarette smoke is everywhere. The Marines smoke. Many women Marines smoke, often rationalizing that it is only because of the stress of the war zone. It is impossible to get away from second-hand smoke, and when I tell them that more and more of the civilized world is banning smoking, they just look at me..."whatever." I wish they would not smoke. I want them to live forever.

9

THE MEMORIES

My memories of being in Iraq with these incredible Marines are crowded with conflicting thoughts of anxiety, when I realized that I was in great danger, and the hard work of traveling alone in a country where I was definitely an outsider. I had no driver, no cameraman, no interpreter, and no commanding officer. The anxiety always quickly abated when I was swept up in my mission. As with the Marines I interviewed, I was so elated to be in Iraq, so focused on what was happening next, and so concentrated on doing the job right that worry about being in danger was pushed to the back of my mind.

I have traveled alone in several foreign countries, often where my command of the language was minimal. I always managed, by keeping my wits, and working backward from a "worst-case" scenario, to come through the most trying circumstances safely. Never, however, have I been in physical danger, in harm's way, as I was in Iraq.

1stLt Sara Hope is OIC of the volunteer FSF.

You wouldn't believe the work I've been doing for the past two months putting this detachment of female Marines together. I have learned more in the last two months than probably my entire time in the Marine Corps. The group of females [in the FSF] is great. I was just blown away. They all volunteered, and I'm talking very high-quality Marines. They were motivated every day no matter how crappy it was outside. They knew what they were doing was important. They were so enthusiastic, so professional. And we were out there working with grunts and artillerymen and Marines that have never worked with women before—and all I ever got from these guys was compliments for my Marines. "Hey! Your Marines are awesome!" It just meant a lot to me. We knew that what we were training to do was making a difference, and being part of operations [preparing to move into a combat zone] was great. My job in administration is important, and I love my battalion and I love the Marines I work with, but being out there and doing the other thing—I mean leading Marines in combat is pretty much every Marine officer's goal—this is as close as I'm going to get. The pride I had in these Marines preparing for this role is something I'll remember for a long, long time. It's pretty much the pinnacle of my career so far, and I'm sure it will continue to be for awhile. It was awesome.

CWO4 Kim Adamson will carry away with her the memory of being involved with the Iraqis in the setup of a court system in Fallujah.

Just being here, seeing the Marines, the teamwork, the first free elections in decades, just being part of the emerging democracy in the country, it's something. The same Marines who are in combat operations can change that quick and become humanitarians in minutes—helping the people. It's very unique.

1stLt Blanca Binstock, as a public affairs officer, has often been present in the States when Marines return home from a deployment in Iraq.

I always wonder, when I look at really young Marines, what's going through their minds, what's their story. I know they do such awesome things over here, and I feel so proud of them. I really am. In the rear, one of the special things I do is invite the media to come when our Marines are coming home. I see the families and think of their sacrifices and I get choked up, standing there, watching.

I don't have any children yet. We've been married ten years, but I wanted to do this—to deploy to the war. I can't imagine leaving a child behind as a father or a mother, or not being there for the birth of your child, or leaving when they're babies and coming back when they're walking and talking. That's such a sacrifice. I've gotten to know some of the spouses of the Marines who are over here. They're just amazing women. I've been in ten years, but these past few years of the war I've really seen what the Marine Corps families go through. I talked to a friend recently who has three daughters, and her husband left [for Iraq] a couple of weeks ago. I told her, "Your job is so much harder than mine is, even being in Fallujah." I can only imagine how strong these women are, back home.

Sgt Lori Luna talks about a young Marine, a lance corporal who, like Sgt Luna, is now a K9 Dog Handler in Iraq.

Before she left [for Iraq], we had a going away for her and she became very emotional with me. I had only known her for a month before she left, but she was very sincere in telling me about the standards I had set for her and how I had made things easier for her as a woman in the Marine Corps. It made me realize that the things we do, even if they are bettering our careers as Marines, are not always just for ourselves, but give confidence and assurance to the younger Marines that follow in your path. When I was a young Marine, I never had someone to look up to; I just made my own path. Hearing that someone looks up to me and is following a path I set out makes me feel almost like an older sister. The Marine women in Iraq are not only affecting a lot of Iraqi women with what they do, they are affecting the world by their actions.

"During my time in the Marine Corps, the greatest thing for me was being a drill instructor," SSgt Alison Arnold tells me.

You'd be surprised how many of these young girls who join the Corps have been abused. It's a great number. These girls have been either verbally or physically or sexually abused, and you see them come to boot camp with no confidence whatsoever, completely down on their luck.

When they leave, they're feeling on top of the world, that they can take on anyone, anything that gets in their way. They make it as a team. That's everything that they're being taught. That, for me, is the most rewarding thing. I'd see a new group of girls go through every three months.

Other things I remember are when I was a sergeant, doing my job as a radio operator, and my unit would go out with the infantry, co-locate with infantry headquarters, and I'd be the only female. We'd go out for 30 days at a time, and I was just doing my job, as usual. There was a major with the infantry communications unit who didn't like me. When he saw me he said, "What are you doing out here? I don't think you need to be out here." It was an attitude, like "You don't belong here." I just said, "Okay, well, you know, sir, I'm here. I've got my job to do." A couple of days later he came up to me and had one of his radios that was broken and he couldn't get communications with anybody. I was the only one around, so he said, "Fix my radio." I looked at it and saw it was something simple and I fixed it in, like, two seconds and he had comm again. He just shook his head and told me, "You know what? I still don't think you should be out here, but I'll take you with me any day." He made me feel appreciated. He made me feel good about myself, like I *did* belong. I think the situation that's emerging here will change a lot of things for females.

1stSgt Patrice Arline tells me that seeing women Marines in Iraq, completely dedicated to their mission, reminds her of her most satisfying role as drill sergeant, training women Marines.

Something that sticks in my mind all the time is an experience I had at Parris Island as a drill instructor. You really don't know how you affect other people. You don't know that is your purpose, what you're supposed to do. When I was in drill instructor school, I kept thinking *I'm too old*. I was 30 years old. *I'm too old to do this. Why am I doing this at this point in my career?* I felt that this question was answered for me while I was there. There was a recruit who always had her head down. It was almost as if she wouldn't walk next to you. I mean, she couldn't walk next to me. She always had this attitude of hanging back and holding her head down. I would always tell her, "Pick your head up. You don't want anyone to take that pride away from you." She would tell me, "It's really a cultural thing." I didn't know anything about that—how much of that was true, but I just kept saying it anyway, "Hold your head up." On graduation day, somewhere she got this card she gave me, and I've kept that card to this day. She wrote in there that she didn't really know why she joined the Marines and was going to boot camp. She wasn't getting along with her parents. But she was glad she did it because I said something to her that has changed her life. So from that day forward she would hold her head up, even if she was going through a bad time. She listed all the situations where she would always hold her head up and she wouldn't let anyone take that away from her.

Years later, she found me, even though my name had changed. She told me she's still holding her head up. You don't know how much that meant. It's these instances and these young women that you have a chance to reach out and touch. That's awesome. That's the drill instructor experience. You see on TV and in the movies, the drill instructors yelling in your face, but the impact you have on these young lives is just big—it's huge. So I always think about the recruits, all the time. What it took for them to get there. And I kept that card, because just as I was asking myself, "Why am I here? What am I doing?" she was asking herself the same thing, "Why am I here?" It was the same question. Through it all, thick or thin, if I win or I lose, I'm going to hold my head up.

When you're a drill instructor you don't really see the effects of it because you move among so many recruits and you progress, and you're growing as much as they're growing. In the end, at graduation, you can stand back and see the product. Boot camp, I always say, is the only organization that can make the biggest change in the shortest time. Some of the kids come there with so many issues. We talk about core values a lot. You listen to them talk about how they've never had more than one or two pairs of new shoes in their life, and now they're in boot camp and they've got these two pairs of boots and a new pair of running shoes. They have several changes of clothes. Seeing that is so profound.

Boot camp isn't for everybody. Some of them just don't make it. I believe you really have to want to make it, because it's easy to give up. It's really tough. It's all hurry-up, rushing to eat, rushing to get dressed—you gain strength from that. And what do you learn about time management? It isn't easy to see it then. But you've got a schedule, you've got all these people to get to chow, and everybody can't take their time. You would never get there! So it's not for everybody. And that's not a bad thing, if they don't make it.

The girls come from all walks of life. Some of them have been gang members. Some of them have been the victims of incest. Some of them have been raped. So psychologically, it's tough when you have someone yelling at you when you've already been beat down by other people. Some of them just don't make it. And some of them resist. They've grown up in neighborhoods where you don't want people in your face. It's hard for them to come to grips with the fact that this is just boot camp, a three-month training period. That isn't really clear.

1stSgt Laura Brown relates how her Marines make her proud.

Last year, when we were getting ready to deploy, I got yanked from my unit on a Military Police company, probably a week before we were getting ready to go to the line of departure. That pained me. This group of men—I called them Neanderthals, were all Type A personalities. It was funny. They were all very opinionated. But the bottom line was always mine. I told them, "I'll listen to you, but at the end, shut up. It's what I say and that's how we're going to do it, and that's what I'll say to the CO." It always worked, but they never said they appreciated me, never, ever. It was always good-natured bantering. Then when I got yanked out and it was time for me to leave, I saw these men with tears in their eyes, and that was amazing to me. That was just huge to me. That was an incident I can't forget.

About three weeks ago, out here, my XO passed away. A mortar landed on him. That changed me, because last year when I met him, I didn't realize I was in the presence of an angel. I thought he was just a nice guy. But he was amazing. He never got bent out of shape. Everything rolled off his back. I consider myself a child of God, so I try not to get bent, but I do. This guy, he was just amazing. I had seen him a week before he passed away. We were talking and laughing, and then he was gone, instantly. It was difficult. But what it said to me was, "Don't take things for granted." You never know when you're in the presence of angels, and he was one of them.

You see the younger generation now, and people who look like me, Hispanic young women. I was coming out of the chow hall one day and someone asked, "Ma'am, can we take a picture with you?" I asked them, "Do I know you?" and they said, "No, ma'am." I just started laughing, because I remember that back in my day, when I was their age, there wasn't anyone that looked like me. But to them I represented someone they wanted to be like. It's because I'm a First Sergeant and I'm Hispanic and I'm a woman. So I said, "Okay, let's do it," and they took the picture.

SgtMaj Suzanne How has many memories about interacting with Marines at all levels in Iraq. She's surprised that Marines also remember her.

Two years after we left Iraq the first time, one of my young sergeants wrote me an e-mail saying, "I just want to thank you for your years of service. I never had a woman lead me before, and you really changed my outlook on everything, not just women. You taught me so much about leadership. I want to thank you." Some come up to me and tell me I really make them feel like a person, that I really touched them. They're not necessarily my Marines, they're just someone you see—at chow, even in the shower. I talk to them and ask them about their lives, back home, and what's going on. Around here you forget those kinds of things. You don't realize there's another life.

As a woman, Cpl Michelle Garza senses the caring side of the Marines she serves with.

I know when I go outside the wire, they worry. Of course, everyone worries when anybody goes past the wire, but one time when I went on a convoy on a buying operation, I didn't come back that night, but came back the next morning instead. They told me my lieutenant didn't sleep because he was worried. The people I work with are like family. I don't know what it'll be like when we leave here because you see the same people every day. It's a different kind of bond when you're out here. It's not like working in the rear, at home.

Capt Jennifer Morris remembers many instances of heroism that impressed her—heroes both Iraqi and American.

In town, an Iraqi pointed out a car and informed one of the Marines that there was a man and woman inside, and the car was going to explode. The Marines went to check on it and could see the man, but he was slumped over. The woman looked like she was alive. The car was supposedly going to blow up at any moment. But the Marines got the woman out of the car and just minutes later the car went up in a huge explosion. They got the woman out, but she died soon after. She had been shot. Both the man and woman had been shot and left there in a car full of explosives. The people in the village were cheering. They couldn't believe it. They thought it was unbelievable that the Marines would risk their lives to try to save an Iraqi woman in a situation like that.

Most inspiring is the fact that people voted. Election Day was amazing. I had a feeling of dread about that day and worried that there would be absolute violence. I thought no one would come out and vote, that they'd be too afraid. When we went into the city, to the command post, we had a big board updating voting numbers at all the polling sites. And the numbers kept coming in. The people came out and voted. There were mortar attacks, and they run away and then come back after the smoke cleared. I was so impressed. I mean, I know Americans who don't bother to vote in the safety of their hometowns. And these people are coming out. They may not completely understand why they're voting, but they did it.

1stLt Alexandra Plucinski shares some moving experiences with me that tell a lot about the things Marines absorb without being taught.

We don't get a lot of feedback as officers. You get feedback if you're messing up. And if you do an outstanding job, at the end of your deployment or your billet, you'll get awards. But as you go along day to day, you never really know. You speak with your peers often, and I can ask my platoon sergeant, "Is there anything you're not getting from me?"

There was an incident when we were on a convoy. One of my corporals was my driver for the day and there was a problem with gear coming off one of the trucks, and we had to get that off-loaded. The Marine who was driving the truck didn't belong to our unit, wasn't in our platoon. He was just not doing his job as driver and being part of the team. So I called him over and he walked across to me with his hands in his pockets. When your officer calls you, your lieutenant calls you, you better be running. I chewed his ass for about five minutes about how he needed to step up and show responsibility. And if he didn't know how to do his job, we'd get somebody to replace him. I told him his conduct was pulling the entire convoy down. I was focused on just getting things done right and getting the mission done.

That night we got back after a long, long, long day and I hear my corporal yelling at this guy. I didn't want to interfere because they handle things on their own level. I didn't want to get involved. I heard my corporal tell him, "You're a piece of crap. How dare you not operate on the level of the platoon when you're with a new unit? You're not carrying your own weight. What's wrong with you? If you ever walk when my lieutenant calls you again, I'm going to kick your ass!" Hearing him say "my lieutenant" and telling him how he should respect me, that just, to me, it just meant a lot.

Another time, on another convoy, we were delivering pallets of bottled water. A lot of times the pallets break apart very easily. They often load them wrong and they break apart. It's a pain in the butt to deliver water because of that. At one area, we were dropping off water and the pallets broke, and there were hundreds of bottles of water all over the deck. I think it was one early stop out of eight we had to do that day, so there wasn't enough time to do anything. You can't restack it. It was already established that if the pallets break, it's not our fault. We delivered it, you can work with it. So the XO comes out of his command center and starts yelling at the Marines. They had just piled everything in one area. "You can't leave this water here! This is not professional. If you do a job, you finish, you complete the job." I told him we had a lot of deliveries to make that day and we can't take the time, but he just started going off on them. So I told him, "It's not their job. A pallet breaks. This happens quite frequently. We're sorry for the inconvenience, but there's a hands-off rule about stacking boxes of water, bottled water, by hand." We didn't have any forks with us that day. They were already tired and this was just one stop of many we were going to do that day. I said, "They can't do it. This is a not a working party. We've got to be on the run." We had a few words back and forth and finally he said, "Okay, whatever." He was pissed off.

Later that night when we got back, we debriefed. We gather all the Marines around and we talk about the good points and the bad points of the mission and improvements they can work on. One PFC spoke up. He'd gotten into trouble before, but he's a good Marine; he just lets his mouth go sometimes. He said, "I want to thank you for sticking up for us today, because if you weren't there, they'd have made us clean up that mess. And we'd have been late. You all don't see that, but she sticks up for us a lot and she goes to bat for us, so I want to just thank her for that." I was sitting there thinking *Okay, don't overdo it.* After the debriefing, he came up to me and said, "We get screwed over a lot. We appreciate it when you stick up for us." So—you don't need recognition, but when you get it, it's nice.

At one point we were transporting detainees. The battle was kicking off and there were mortar rounds exploding all around us. We were on edge. We were trying to get moving because of the risk of getting blown up. We have a protocol for what we do throughout our chain of command. One thing is that if two detainees know each other and are talking, they're not allowed to be together. We don't want them talking and not following commands and getting fired at. I had an old man come up to me, smiling at me. I asked the translator what was wrong, because the detainees usually don't approach me. Through the translator I found out that the old man's son was on the other truck. He was asking me, with tears in his eyes, "Please, can I be with my son? I stopped for a moment. I thought *My dad is Israeli. He lost his whole family to the Holocaust. They were taken away like this and he was separated from his family. I'm dealing with people who are being taken away, and I'm separating this family.* These detainees were not being detained for no reason. It's not that type of situation. We're not going to torture them or kill them. I've seen the facilities myself. But the old man doesn't know this. And the emotional part of me is saying, "How can you do this? How are you going to tell this man that you have to separate him from his son?" Then I looked at the man and I told him that he had to get on the truck, but when he got to the facility, he'd be with his son. It would only be about an hour they'd be separated. So I felt I'd done the right thing. I'm not obligated to explain anything to any of them. But it did make me stop and think *What would they think if they knew a half-Israeli woman, with Jewish upbringing, was telling them what to do?*

LtCol Lori Reynolds feels strongly that her Marines will retain a lot of the lessons they learned in Iraq.

There's not a lot of heroics out here. It's just the day-to-day mission. But when they go back, we try to make the point that what they learned here can change their lives. They can say they went for seven months without alcohol and lived through it, because that is definitely a problem back there. A lot of these kids are away from mom and dad for the first time. There's a lot of temptation for these kids back in southern California. There's Mexico right down the road. Everything's expensive. In the rear, you spend too much time dealing with family problems. This one's just left his wife because they've never been taught how to deal with problems, how to respect each other. They were fighting all the time. I tell him that I grew up, for 18 years with my mom and dad, and the cops never came to my house because mom and dad were arguing. I learned that from them. My eyes were really opened in recruiting as to where some of these kids come from. We don't just train them how to communicate here. You also train them how to take care of a family, what's proper behavior. To me it's a readiness issue.

The job of a commanding officer now is more than just getting the mission done. The smart kids take care of that. What I'm learning is that everybody's important, so you have to deal with family issues. You have to remove obstacles for them. My concern is that after a deployment like this they'll say, "Okay, I did my part," and they'll get out. Many of these kids have been through OIF-I and OIF-II (Operation Iraqi Freedom 1 and 2) and they might feel they've done their part. Once you get a big deployment like this, where you're part of something big, and they know they did well, they might say, "I'm ready to do something else." That's when you really start talking about the intangibles of the Corps and making sure they're feeling those intangibles are important in their lives.

Sometimes they realize that later and come back in. One of my Marines did that. He was an infantryman, wanted to go to war, wanted to do something big, and it just wasn't happening. Then his wife got pregnant and he said, "I've got to take care of my family." Then 9/11 happened and he said, "This is my war," so he came back. Wanted to be an infantryman, but he ended up here in communications. There's a lot of patriotism.

I don't think people get that about patriotism. Everybody volunteered to be here. This is the big show for them. You've just got to keep them focused. I love to read about Civil War battles. I constantly wonder, like Pickett's charge—I mean, there were 150,000 men and they told them, "Go face that cannon." How did they get those guys to walk across that field? How in the world, when they saw those cannons facing them, did they walk straight towards them? How do you get guys to do that? I don't think our challenge is nearly that great here, but it's the same thing at stake. They've got to be proud of what they do. They've got to know they're here for a reason. They've got to be well led.

It has to do with their job. I didn't really learn this until I was a captain, but they want to understand. It's just communications. Comm is what we do. "That's the hill, go set up on that hill." But when you explain what's going on and what their part in all this is, they understand and they do it better. For instance, there's a hot spot near Karbala. The Sunnis aren't happy. So we've got to make sure that comm to Karbala is good. So when they know "Okay, that's why the field's worried about comm," they do it better. They want to learn. I want them to ask questions. I've learned so much about just the common everyday types of things that they're thinking. The bottom line is these are all good kids who came in for a good reason, and you've just got to keep teaching them. It's a great job. I don't know how I got this job, but it's a great job.

These kids are really good. When you're back home, you worry about the generation coming up. Rap music, violence, videos, it's just—but I don't worry about it out here. When you see their potential and you take them out of that environment, it's amazing. I'll tell you a story about these kids. When we got here, there was a group of Filipino girls that were working in the chow halls. These gals—I mean, how bad must it be in the Philippines for them to come to Fallujah, Iraq, to work? They lived in a little trailer right here next to us. They were saving all their pay until they can go home. One day the trailer burned down, and they lost everything, their clothes, and all that money. So my Marines raised money for them. In the middle of everything, we were dodging bullets, and they're taking up a collection for them. All on their own. Compare that to just a random group of 19- or 20-year-old kids back home. Back home where we like to think we really care about people. It was a completely positive experience coming out here, you know, because when you get back home, you have all the temptations again.

LCpl Crystal Groves tells me a story about being commended by her sergeant.

In MOS school, I ended up in the hospital for about a week. And I was dropped from my class because of that. I was raised a good kid. I'd never been in trouble my whole life, never been in any trouble at all. I stayed in the barracks. I did what I was supposed to do. I did my classes. I studied at night. But I ended up getting dropped. I didn't like my staff sergeant. There was something about him. One time he had a PT (physical training) session, and I don't know if he was mad or what, but out of 48 of us, only 9 didn't fall out. It killed a lot of people, but I stuck in there. This sergeant came to the hospital every day I was in there. I'll never forget what he told me. He said, "I don't know why this had to happen to a Marine like you. Because I was a loner like you. I could relate." I didn't realize he had any respect for me. I was like, wow!

2ndLt Samantha Kronschnabel says she often writes home about her Marines because "they're funny. They make me laugh." She also finds some of the experiences they share with her very touching.

Once I picked up the platoon, and we were getting ready to deploy, so I had everybody write a biography so I could learn a little bit about them. They all wrote at least three pages about themselves, and that's a big deal for Marines. They haven't written since high school. Some of them haven't graduated high school. Some are better writers than others, but they wrote, and they don't hesitate to open up about their families, their home lives, how they were picked on in high school, how they were overweight in high school, how their father beat them—broken, broken things. Writing about themselves. To read these pages and to see how they just grew, got out of their bad situations, whatever it was, and came into the Marine Corps, and are doing the things we do everyday—so important—it brings tears to your eyes. How strong these young Marines are! And they're 17, 18, 19. I hope they'll hang onto these values when they get out. I think they will. I think they will. Like the motto says, the change is forever. I think it is.

LtCol Cindy Atkins recalls a Marine who worked for her in San Diego before she retired and was later recalled from retirement to deploy to Iraq.

He had done his four years and got out. The Marines Corps called him back to be a combat replacement and he said, "Sure." I bumped into him as we were getting ready to fly out here from the States. He knew I had retired. I never knew what happened to him, but here we were together, getting ready to fly out. I always called him "my" Marine because he'd worked for me, and so I told him that if he got stuck in downtown Fallujah, he should come get me; "I don't care what time of day or night it is, come get me." Well, later when we thought the Battle of Fallujah was pretty much over and cleaned up, one Sunday afternoon I was sitting at my desk and I got a call. I get what's called a spot report for all the wounded. They sent an e-mail that someone is being treated and it's my Marine. It said "Shrapnel wounds in hand." So I thought *it's just his hand.* But I decided to go down and see how he's doing.

I went down and ran into the sergeant major for the battalion and asked him how he was doing. He told me, "We lost five tonight." I had not realized it had gotten that heated. I told him I was sorry about the losses and asked if there was anything we could do. "Pray for us," is what he said. Then the first sergeant came out and told me they'd had losses and several wounded. I told him that's why I was there. They told me they were going back out. "We're going to go get them."

Then I went inside. It was dreadful. They had lost five Marines, but I bet 10 to 15 were coming into triage. I looked on the chart and saw my Marine was in Ward 7. It was full of Marines. Everywhere there was blood and bandages. I saw him. They had just brought him in. They were trying to get an IV in. His right leg was bandaged. He was obviously very agitated. I sat on the cot with him. The Corpsman was trying to get him to calm down and was giving him morphine to ease the pain. When he saw me I said, "Hey, you're going to be okay." But he said, "Ma'am, you've got to find the corporal." I asked him to tell me about the corporal. He said, "He was up at the top of the stairs and that's the last I saw of him. All he had was his pistol. You've got to find the corporal." Here I was talking to a Marine who's bandaged and upset about his buddy, and I had to try not to be emotional. All around me were injured Marines.

I went running down the hall, looking at charts trying to find the corporal. He wasn't listed on anything. I went down to the office and they suggested I check MA, mortuary affairs. I couldn't do that. I thought *I'm not going to go there.* So I went back to my Marine and told him the corporal wasn't here and that we'd just have to go find him. He started telling me about what happened in the house. They went up the stairs and the bad guys were up top. They had a good angle. Grenades starting coming in and everything was exploding all over the place. They were firing AK-47s. He just kept telling me, "You've got to find him." Here's this Marine, badly shot in the leg, been through all this, and all he's worried about is another Marine. It was so touching.

I began helping with other Marines in the ward. Half the platoon was in there. But he was so worried about his buddy. He wasn't worried about himself, only making sure his buddy was okay. One Marine next to him had shrapnel all over his back. Another's leg had been all shot up. Another Marine had no backside. They had a plastic sheet over him and he was shivering. His ankles were hurting because he was lying on his side because his backside was all shot up. I got a pillow and put it between his feet. It was chaotic, but the medical staff was amazing. They triaged everybody and got the ones into surgery who needed it first. It's amazing how they figure out who's going to live that they can put morphine into, calm them down, and work on the ones where they may need to save a limb. They saved a lot of limbs.

The shot went through the back of his leg. He was on the stairs going up in the house—they were able to piece it together as the days went by. I'd go down every night and check on them, bring them Gatorade, just see if they needed anything. The grenade apparently knocked him off the stairs and his buddies dragged him out. He had no shrapnel; it was a clean shot to the back of his leg. I found out the next day that the corporal, his buddy, didn't make it. I was going to go tell him but when I got down there I just couldn't do it. The company commander came by and helped him fill in the gaps in his memory as to what happened. He remembers being on the stairs and his buddies dragging him out, but that's all he remembers. Apparently what had happened to his buddy was, he was at the top of the stairs and the bad guys started firing. He backed into a room, only to back into a whole bunch of bad guys. It was horrible.

When my Marine got back to the States, to California, he e-mailed me that they think he got a broken vertebra from being knocked off the stairs. He was a fireman before he came back in, and he e-mailed that the firemen had a big welcome home party for him and that they spend a lot of time with him. He is happy to be back with his wife. They have a little girl. The news people want to do a story on him and he wrote to me, "I don't have a story to tell." I answered him, "Oh, yes you do."

In the ward with him there was a Marine across from him that had been shot up pretty good in his arm. It was the third time he'd been injured. They told him he wouldn't be coming back this time. They told him they'd medivac him to Germany and then home. He complained that he had orders to go to the drill field, and he didn't want the orders to the drill field canceled. He wanted to go be a drill instructor. I told him, "You'll get there."

Another of the wounded was a lance corporal, a cook. He wasn't even an infantryman. But he was needed and so the staff sergeant pulled him into the QRF, Quick Reaction Force, as lance corporal. He was proud of that. He told me his father and grandfather had both been Marines. His head and arms were all bandaged. The staff sergeant continued to motivate him, telling him, "You're one of us. You're part of us. You're my combat cook." They're all shot up and they're still being encouraged. That's the kind of stuff that's just, you know, it's heartwarming, and at the same time, sad. These are young boys. I worry about my own Marines, just watching the paperwork come through and thinking...

The Commandant has issued a new policy. It used to be that they'd go talk with these wounded Marines and medically retire them. Now the Commandant is saying they will keep as many in as they can, if they want to stay. "We'll figure out a way for them to fit in." So we have that now. There is a Marine colonel who was wounded in Grenada and lost part of his leg and part of an arm. He was a pilot. He doesn't fly, but he stayed in and made it to colonel. He's in intel.

These Marines have sacrificed. I hope the Marine Corps will establish programs to try to stay in touch with these Marines, so they can be around other Marines and have Marine family to take care of them. There are so many organizations that have popped up, nonprofits, that are out here supporting us. I'll tell you, the American public has been very supportive. They weren't around when Vietnam was over, when the troops came home from Vietnam. It was ugly then. What a difference here.

The most profound experience of Col Jenny Holbert's deployment in Iraq, and her strongest memory, is sending Marine combat correspondents into Al Fajr—the Battle of Falljuah. She established an unprecedented principle of sending as many correspondents and journalists as could be supported and wanted to go—72 in all. All, she felt, were needed to tell the story of the Urban Operation that was Al Fajr.

Al Fajr was fought block by block through the large city. For the first time ever, Col Holbert placed three combat correspondents in each battalion, instead of one. There were 45 or more civilian media representatives from newspapers or TV and radio, with video and still cameras, and laptops.

During the battle, Humvees heading into the battle would stop by the PA office to pick up reporters. The reporters could choose not to go; the Marine combat correspondents were assigned to go by Col Holbert. She found it the most profound experience of her tour of duty, to send Marine combat correspondents into Fallujah. "I felt their parents sitting on my shoulder," she said, and hoped she was making the right decision.

Near the end of the battle, Col Holbert went "downtown" into Fallujah. She remembers seeing portions of the city, where houses had made up a busy neighborhood, looking like a landfill.

> It was empty—the city was quiet and empty. It was a bright, warm day, and the only movement was the dust blowing and dogs wandering about. It was like a ghost town.
>
> In the northwest quadrant, a residential area, the houses were still intact, but every other block or so had a row of houses and then, next door, a pile of rubble, where a house was destroyed. There was no color in the city, just a monotone of gradations of brown. Dust covered everything.
>
> In the business section, a triangle formed by roads that converged at the Euphrates River, many businesses were still untouched. There was a formal wear shop, with display windows blown out, but like a shop in a small town in Iowa, the mannequin still posed in the window in a full-skirted formal gown, with lace. The colors were muted with dust. In a men's shoe store, there were shelves of shoes, all neatly lined up with the heels back, toes to the front, all the color of dust. The cash register was untouched. There was no looting. Nearby a shop had rows of shirts hung on racks against the wall, all neatly arranged. It was like pictures you see of a disaster, but no evidence of flooding or collapse, just emptiness and dust.
>
> In early spring we began to see color in the city—piles of oranges and lemons and colorful clothing on the people. The city was coming back.

10

COMING HOME

Coming home from war is a shock. It can be a relief, a wrench, a joyful reunion, a lonely adjustment, a huge letdown, and/or a cause for celebration. Marines who come home from war without being wounded look like the Marines who went to war, but there has been a big change, often indiscernible, even to close family members.

A war zone is a different world, without privacy, freedom of movement, with scant personal initiative, and with an urgent, ubiquitous sense of danger. This would seem to go without saying, yet the majority of Americans who have no knowledge of war are not really aware of how different it is. Marines, for the most part, suspend thinking about life in the rear, at home. They do not have time to think about bill paying, child rearing, endless options for spending leisure time, and current trends in fashion and politics. Driving your own vehicle, having a hot bath, sending out for pizza, using a drive-thru bank, enjoying a beer after work, or picking up a Starbucks on the way to anywhere is not possible.

Marines put aside those things willingly and talk about them wistfully from time to time, but think of them as delights to be savored in another time and place, when the mission is over. They miss people close to them, but for the first time, in any war, they can talk to those they miss by telephone or communicate by e-mail, daily, if time allows. But what do people talk about when one is at home, wrapped up in the very serious or sometimes banal minutiae of daily life and the other is at risk of his or her life eight time zones away? There is no way to banter about surviving an attack on a patrol or seeing a buddy mangled by a mortar sitting in the vehicle next to you. And the enthusiasm about Johnny winning the track meet or the despair of the washing machine breaking down for the third time in a month is difficult to focus on, given the preoccupation of the Marines on their mission. The focus of each person on the phone or in the e-mail is a world away, and all that remains is the beloved sound of a voice or caring words that are timeless.

When Marines have been deployed for half a year or more, the world they are in takes more and more precedence over the world they left behind to the point where it can be a strain to recapture the civilian point of view as a father, daughter, mother, or son, even for the length of a phone call. You become a different person. Going back to the person you were, the person those at home identify with, sometimes becomes very difficult.

Marines serving in Iraq become what they have been trained to be: professional, dedicated to the mission, and totally focused on the job at hand. They are riflemen, commanding officers, platoon leaders, drivers, infantrymen, clerks, radio operators, disbursing clerks, logistics personnel, force reconnaissance, pilots, mechanics, cooks, communications and intelligence experts, or one of a hundred other Military Operational Specialties. But they are all in Iraq for one reason: to fight a war, or to support those who are pulling the triggers. They are finally, after months of tough training, and intense schooling, doing the job they have been taught to do, a job many get to do only after years of service: being in a war.

The Marines I spoke with would not trade their part in the Iraq War for anything, even though the guilt of parting with family members is sometimes extremely difficult to live with. The demands of the job erase all other considerations. Rising early, donning regulation uniform, going to chow, heading out to do their job, finding time for physical training, working late, continually training to hone the skills that prepare them for any contingency of war, occupy all their time—from 12 to 17 hours a day, many times even more. Their focus on the mission precludes any other concerns. They are operating at 100 percent efficiency at their jobs. War is what Marines do. When there is no war they train for war. When there is a war, they want to be fighting it, each in his or her own specialty.

When Marines return home, the letdown can be severe. Some weather it well, others not so well. Many are so at odds that they long to go back to the danger. They thrive on it not because they like it so much, but because it demands so much of them. They have to be at their best to survive, and they have all the skills that are necessary to survive as well as to defeat an enemy. They feel most alive when they are doing the job they have been trained for and are excelling. They are a well-honed team that comes alive at times of war, that digs down to the values they have absorbed to function at almost superhuman levels, with every faculty alert and every response inherent and instantaneous. They are the best in the world.

The world at home never demands as much from them. They are not as challenged, their finest skills are unneeded; they are not called upon to be heroes. At home they are no longer a team fighting for survival, or completing a mission; they are training, waiting for their time to go to war again. There are no situations in the civilian world where they are needed, as they are needed in war. There is ambivalence among civilians to honor the dedication and professionalism of the Marines because there is ambivalence about the wars they are called upon to fight.

The Marines are mostly untouched by the politically motivated argument over who supports the troops and who does not. They are too busy, too focused on their mission to pay attention to the latest battle in the war of words back home. They receive care packages and letters from strangers continuously—just ordinary people, whose support leads them to discount what they may hear to the contrary.

This war is like others fought since the end of World War II—far away and not a big deal on civilian radar screens. The number of men and women serving in the U.S. military is less than one-half of 1 percent of our population. The majority of those are quartered around 200 military bases in the United States where the awareness of the Iraq War is high. In the States, Marines live and operate in a segregated society—those serving and connected to the military and those who are not. The Internet has done more to raise the consciousness of ordinary Americans about Marines and the war they are fighting than all the other media.

For millennia, service in the military has been an honored tradition in our Western heritage. Beginning with the Greeks, and throughout history, the military has been one of the preferred occupations among the titled, the educated, and the upper classes. The merchant class was not considered as a highly respected profession. With the development of global economies and the American notion of individual freedom and entrepreneurialism, military service has now taken a back seat to the production of wealth. There are no year-end bonuses or stock options in the military. The pay scale and the extra pay—for combat or per diem or disability or other—is not considered high, and the amounts are available as public knowledge.

While Marines are often heroes, they are also humans, subject to mistakes and errors of judgment. If they are held to a higher standard, it is because of their rigorous training in the values of honor, courage, and commitment. We have come to expect them to be as they appear—noble warriors. Their errors are of an exponentially larger nature when they are dealing with human lives.

They are strenuously and meticulously trained and then pitted against an enemy that recognizes none of their morals or values. In this recent war, the enemy has shown a devastating willingness to sacrifice their own lives to create havoc. A suicide bomber leaves no enemy for Marines to advance against. The enemy is mostly indistinguishable from civilians —an enemy that does not value human life in the way that Marines do. Often women and children are used as shields or suicide bombers or blackmailed to become combatants themselves. This goes to the very heart of Marine Corps training. Who is the enemy and who are innocent civilians? The enemy wears no distinguishable uniform. The enemy is not easily labeled in any case. The enemy may be foreign fighters aligned with Al Qaeda, Iraqis fighting with Al Qaeda, Sunni Iraqis attacking the mainly Shia Iraqi government, Shia Iraqis against the occupation of Iraq, or fighting back against the Sunni and the military providing security, or any number of small tribal or religious groups.

As I learned in talking to women Marines, great progress is being made in reconstruction, supply, and infrastructure in some areas of the country. But without Marine (or Army) security, all progress is subject to destruction, coupled with reprisals against those Iraqis working with the Coalition forces if our troops are called away to fight elsewhere and insurgents reenter the areas our troops secured. Rotation of troops takes its toll, as well. Crucial diplomacy and agreements made between Marine officers and Iraqis are sometimes nullified when the Marines rotate out and their replacements come in cold, without knowledge of the situation.

Morale continues to be high among Marines due to their intense and constant training. Their focus on the mission overrides all discussion about politics as they concentrate on the work of war. They may disagree in downtime, but they work as a close-knit, nonpolitical team on the job.

The almost constant condemnation of the media for producing only sensational sound bites of horrific events is, oddly, more than balanced by the online world of shared e-mails and blogs that widely circulate the softer stories of heroism, reconstruction, sacrifice, caring, and thoughtfulness among the troops. Poetry, videos, artwork, and community stories extolling the heroics and the sacrifices made by our troops are circulated worldwide, over and over. Gradually, the media are beginning to catch onto this opposing news cache and its appeal to the public. The media have a reputation of being sensationalist among many civilians and Marines.

As for those who feel Marines are loose cannons, drawn to the violence and who ignore the rules of engagement, Marines say: try to understand the enormous pressure, fear, anger, confusion, and shock Marines are subject to in battle and the instantaneous decisions and reactions they are called upon to make. They take a dim view of criticism from those who have never served, and rightly so.

It is why Marine training is so tough, so demanding. If the world had no wars, we would not need Marines. Until the world figures out how to cease warring, I am betting that each American would undoubtedly choose to be on the winning side of any conflict. So the Marines are trained to win, to be the best. But at what cost do we win wars? The cost is enormous, incalculable—to us and to our enemy. The only greater cost to us would be losing.

But what constitutes victory? All Marines I spoke with had ideas about that. They are proud of their new, unofficial MOS—that of being humanitarians. Most of the Marines see victory as giving the Iraqis a chance to live peacefully, to have a better life than they had. Peace is in the hands of the politicians, unfortunately, from the small tribal Sheiks to the elected Iraqis in Baghdad. The Marines have no control over sectarian disagreement and violence. They are asked to provide security to provide a peaceful environment, but there are no clear-cut lines as to who is breaking the peace. The perpetrators are no longer simply foreign insurgents.

The Marines rely on their training and their values to guide them in their actions while they are forward. It is when they rotate out and come home that the confusion takes over. Will they make the Corps their career, or will they get out?

If Marines get out of the Corps when they come home, then they face all the things they had learned to live without in our wild and wooly democracy. They are faced with choices—primarily about jobs, attitude, how to make a living, where to live, and how to survive and compete in a capitalist society. And there are temptations: alcohol, drugs, getting into debt, the wrong friends, gambling, etc.

They have to become fathers, brothers, husbands, wives, mothers, and interact in the challenging give-and-take of relationships when they are primarily used to giving orders, or taking them. They are no longer part of a close-knit team, a unit that will look out for them no matter what. They are separated from the family of Marines they trained with and learned to trust with their lives; they have to find other friends, some who may share their values, some who may not. And they have to find a way to build a life again with family members who are strongly individual and are not automatically a part of a team. The focus turns to other things, other values. They have to operate as an individual again.

The military is not a democracy, nor does it constitute a free, capitalist society. You need your wits about you to succeed in America. Education is key, but it does not guarantee a steady rise to the top. In the military, you succeed by relying on your training, and doing your job well will provide steady promotion. Wealth and power are not goals; honor, professionalism, and service to your country are. It is a simpler world, in a way, because there are fewer options.

Marines tend to make statements about what they believe in that embarrass some people listening to them. Honor, service, dedication, loyalty, and sacrifice are not proactive MBA terms. Young people sometimes mock the values Marines espouse because they are too intense; they are not cool. But when there is a war, the Marines are the ones who go to fight for the rest of us. Then they are heroes. It is a love-hate relationship.

And yet the U.S. military is a powerful force totally under the control of the government and the people it serves. Throughout history, military coups have changed the destinies of many parts of the world, and from the military in many nations have come the most heinous dictatorships known to man. That is not going to happen here. Members of the military have one vote, like all other citizens, and they can voice opposition, write a scathing op-ed piece, mount an Internet protest, or blog in anger, as can anyone, in a nation of free speech. They can choose not to reenlist, and there are some who desert, but they have never gone on strike as a group and refused to fight, and they have never threatened to take over the country.

In essence, they are mostly young people in the line of fire. Nations always send their youngest to war. Some are too young to vote or drink, legally, when they join. Yet they come to understand the dangers and what is expected of them, and they volunteer to serve.

When Marines return home they react to the difference in many ways. Some of the stories I was told indicate their sensitivity to weird occurrences noticeable only to them—they think people are following them, a bunch of leaves in the gutter, an ominous, empty public place. Other stories reflect their disgruntlement with a world that has experienced this war only as one of a dozen news stories in any given day, where many people cannot even locate Iraq on a map or tell you why we are there.

A lieutenant colonel comments,

> When I got home [between deployment in 2004 and again in 2005], I took some time and went back East, to visit all the people who had been reading my e-mails, forwarded from my family. I got to meet these people. I realized people do care. They may not know anyone who's out here, but they were very interested in what I was doing and they do care. There are a lot of people who care. If you say, are there enough of them? I don't know. But for me, it was a very rewarding thing, that people appreciated us.

A corporal says,

> With Marines, it's a different kind of bond than with friends at home. In the rear, you meet people and they become your friends, or maybe not, or co-workers and not so friendly, whatever. You can see them or not, whenever. Sometimes there are conflicts and you don't see them because of some disagreement or something, somebody's mad. But out here, being in a pen with 12 different females, it's different. You work with them, you bond with them, you're with them day and night. Even if you have a hard time getting along with one or two, when someone leaves to go back to the rear, or to another unit, that really sucks. It's sad. I hate good-byes, or even see-you-laters. You meet a lot of good people and then you have to leave. If you really want

to stay in touch, you can, but the war keeps you busy. The world is a busy place.

I still keep in touch with my friends at home, but they don't know what it's like to be here. They don't know what we do, what our job is here. I've been past the wire, and they don't know what that is, what it's like. [When I tell them] they feed off that. They don't understand it, but it's exciting to them. It's dangerous to me. My friends here worry about each other. We talk about that. We talk about everything. My friends at home don't know enough about what's going on out here to know whether to be worried or not.

A sergeant remarks,

When I'm at home, it really saddens me to see people against the war. If they only knew of all the lives lost, allowing for them to have the freedom to protest and express how they feel by voting, picketing, or talking bad about the war. It's hard not to get mad, not easy to bite my tongue. Some people are just ignorant and only care about their simple lives in Smallville. I do, however, appreciate all those who support the troops and grieve for those who are lost.

I've developed a bond with many of my fellow Marines. It's like a sibling bond that I never had. If we're forward, in Iraq, or in the rear, we are protective of each other; we work together and look out for each other.

A first lieutenant states,

I have a real strong, extended family, and I'm in touch with them—even my cousins. Sure, they're proud of me, but they don't really understand what's going on over here. Even my own brother doesn't. They don't know what I do, what I'm dealing with, what the threats are over here. The fact that indirect fire flies in all the time. Until you are here to experience it, you don't get it. It could come whizzing by and take you out at any time. Or how much work we do over here. People who send us things, send board games and playing cards and dominos. I don't mean to denigrate their thoughtfulness, but no one has time out here to sit and do that. You're working 12 to 16 hours a day, and then you've got to find some time to eat, work out—because, as Marines, you've got to stay in shape—and then sleep. Pilots not only fly missions, but we put up the syllabus, and get qualifications, keep training up. You don't have time to goof off here. You make time to write home, because it's important, and e-mail. I try to call home once a week. My mom said one of her friends said, "I didn't realize they were doing so much work over there." What do they think we're doing? Why are we here? There are no weekends over here. There are no days off. You're always working, even if you're not on a mission. You're doing something, planning something, keeping records, getting ready to go. One of my cousins sent me an e-mail that said, "Thank goodness you guys aren't taking mortars." And that morning we had a mortar attack. It doesn't dawn on them. They don't see it on the news, so it's not happening.

A sergeant adds,

Back home, it's hard to accept how focused on themselves everybody is. They don't realize how privileged they are—how much they take for granted. There is misperception about how everything is over here. It's reported as so negative. All the good work with the Iraqis, people don't hear about.

A lieutenant colonel says,

I know that even if we're laughing and joking and we don't act like it, we're all under tremendous stress. Most folks don't realize until the first time they go home. Then they'll hear a noise, or something will trigger a response and your heart will skip a few beats. Then you look around and say, "Oh, okay, I'm home." And then you settle down. That's just the way it is over here. You try not to think too much about what's going on at home because of what you've got going on here. We're in our own little world. I think the most news any of us really gets is when we go over to the chow hall and happen to listen to either Fox or BBC. You realize your stress level when you get home, not when you're here. It affects people in many ways. People have trouble getting over sickness. It's not unusual to have an ordinary cold for two months. You don't sleep regularly. You get gray hair. When I went home last time I was only home a couple of days, but that's where you start feeling everything. Right now we're just sucking it up to get through, one way or another. It doesn't matter how.

A first lieutenant explains,

One thing I think many vets go through, and I'm sure I'll probably be no exception, is the inability to "turn off" deployment mode. I remember the bus ride back from March Air Base, our point of reentry into the States, and freaking out because there were civilian cars so close to the bus. Any civilian vehicles within 50 feet of us in Iraq we were allowed to engage. Every time I was on the road, an unconscious panic set in. I had such pain in my jaw that I had to see the dentist when I got back. He asked me if I had recently been in a "stressful situation" because I was clenching my teeth together so hard. I was also grinding my teeth in my sleep. Even today, when I am in a tight situation, I don't realize it, but my jaw tightens immediately.

Loud noises startle me. Last year, when I was at home on vacation with my boyfriend, we were sitting in a bar in Mexico when someone began shooting off fireworks. We laughed when we both found ourselves under the table. If a door bangs, or anything gets dropped, or anything loud on the road, it immediately triggers something in me that gets my heart pounding and my awareness is heightened. I notice every little thing. In the rear I sometimes drove straddling both lanes, and swerving to avoid every piece of trash or clump of brush on the road. I'm thinking *IED!* I still swerve, but manage to stay in my own lane.

I went through a depression when I got back. My marriage was failing, and we had been apart too long. But I felt as if I needed someone and was angry that he couldn't provide me with the support I needed. My platoon scattered to the wind. The battalion started moving Marines around. The bond was broken.

A captain states,

I found going home to be frustrating. After the initial excitement of seeing my family and friends, I found I was annoyed at the complacency and ignorance about the war in most people. It annoyed me that they worried about such insignificant things and seemed oblivious to what was going on elsewhere in the world. I wanted to go back to Iraq and felt that only there would I be doing a fulfilling job and contributing to a greater good. I'm a Reservist and will be returning to Iraq, but meanwhile I took a government job in Intelligence. That helped. I couldn't look seriously at civilian jobs where I wouldn't be contributing to the war effort. The TV and the news still aggravate me, and I constantly remind myself that they don't tell the whole story.

It's been very difficult to explain these feelings to our families and non-military friends. For some reason, I feel guilty not going back to do our job... the job we were trained to do. I feel like I haven't done enough. I'm so glad I went to Iraq as a Marine and that I had the experience to be a part of history. I really don't think I could ever have a job more rewarding.

A first lieutenant adds,

I had a minor in women's studies, and I was a publicist before I came into the Marine Corps. How teenage girls dominate the market boggles my mind. And also how so many of the things our lives revolve around today were things we women experienced silently as girls, not in-your-face the way many teens do today. Most unnerving is what teenagers, especially girls, are like today. I don't know if it's just me as an individual, as a female Marine with combat experience, or just an older, wiser version of myself, but I am disgusted by much of what I see in teenagers, and especially the girls. I kind of remember being put off, as a teen, with the girls who were so into makeup and boys and clothes, but I don't remember being as angry as I am today. Now, when I see teenagers in the malls and stores, see how disrespectful and oblivious they are to everything around them—local and internationally—I am sickened.

The young men and women who come into the military obviously already have a sense of duty or they wouldn't join. But I wonder about the other kids nowadays. I hear arguments from both the left and right that our children deserve a childhood, and they shouldn't be exposed to life's horrors. But we, as a nation, are so far removed from the horrors of war that are taking the lives of our men and women in uniform, that it seems the least they could do is have some decency to recognize that sacrifice and keep the trite crap to a minimum. Maybe it's just me as a vet talking, but it seems it's also their parents. They have to keep the world real for those kids. The kids seem to have no sense of sacrifice, of compromise, of feeling that others are laying their lives on the line for them. I'd like to think that Americans have some sense of how privileged and luxurious their lives are, but I see no acknowledgment of that.

My father is Israeli and my mother is from the Philippines. When I was 17 we went to Israel to see my father's homeland and visit family. I was bored— no 17-year-old wants to hang out with their parents on vacation—and was looking for someone to party with. It suddenly dawned on me that all the soldiers I saw were my Israeli peers. They were teenagers. It is an obligation for Israeli citizens to honor and fight (in various, different ways) for the survival of their country. Why can't we have that here? Not a draft, don't misunderstand me, but to give our young people a sense of responsibility and awareness of the rest of the world—how volatile, fragile, and violent it can be. Learn not to take your cell phones and the right to wear makeup for granted.

I had an experience in an ice cream shop, when I heard a high-pitched scream and felt someone bump into me. That really heightened my anxiety, and I turned to correct her. I still can go into Marine mode instantly, 24/7, but really try not to around civilians. The girl was probably 15, blond hair done up, a crap-load of makeup on her face. She was dressed in something too tight every way you looked at it—only worn by bad girls when I was that age. She laughed, didn't apologize, and went back to her friends, all hanging on the boys in the group. Their voices were about four octaves higher than I can tolerate. It irritated me to no end. They were giggly, spoke in exaggerated voices, and I wanted to throttle her. I wanted to grab her arm, throw her in a Humvee and take her to see women covered head to toe, following two steps behind their husbands (to whom their marriage was arranged), and carrying everything while the man strolled freely. I wanted to show her the photos of what the Taliban do to women who dare to wear makeup. Or just open a recent issue of *TIME* magazine that tells about the thousands of unaccounted-for Iraqi women who are feared to have been sold into sex slavery and then can't go home when they're rescued because they've disgraced their families, and their families would kill them if they went home.

Would that have an effect? Is this girl one of the reasons that my Marines and I have risked our lives? Yes. It's her choice to act like that, unlike the Arab women who are drugged and taken to work as prostitutes in Dubai. We are Americans because we have choices and freedom. It's an odd dichotomy, the civilian world and the military. I don't think I can ever "think" I am completely safe again. I can't imagine walking down a street and not having the thought of snipers cross my mind. And that's not a bad thing. I am not worse off because I fought this war. I am just different now. I wonder how it will be when I have kids.

A colonel comments,

Being in Iraq, in a war zone, changes your perception of sound. You're in survival mode and everything can be frightening. Even watching fireworks on the Fourth of July, knowing I'm safe at home—it's very uncomfortable. It can trigger memories. Some people repress their emotions while they're in Iraq, and then when they're home, they're tired and angry and don't know why. I catch myself sometimes and realize there's no way to grow when that happens. You have to get above it. But it's difficult. It's a rich life here in the rear. Many times you think they shouldn't be entitled—they haven't paid their dues. It's a soft life, and there's so much safety that people don't even realize it. There is real pain out there and real issues, but people don't seem to want to deal with it. I'm not sure there's any alienation—there's more support for the troops, but the division is on focus. The people of the U.S., not just the military, need to be worried about winning the hearts and minds of the Iraqis. We have to come home, eventually, but the U.S. will be engaged, in one form or another, for a long time to come. There has to be diplomatic, economic, social acceptance, and trust.

In wartime, the military is very engaged. Everything is so real. Decisions can cost lives—it's "success or failure" every day, 24/7, and the issues that come up don't go away. You have to take care of yourself—it's important: eat well, sleep regularly, work out. In the smaller sense, you're wrapped up in the details of the job at hand. In a larger sense, you still wonder, "Why am I here?"

A captain tells me,

One really annoying thing at home is to watch TV and see a report on a suicide bomber, complete with shots of a burning vehicle and panic-stricken or wailing civilians—never, God forbid, any shots of bodies or parts of bodies. It's about a 30-second story, and then there are five minutes or more of civilians editorializing on the situation—mostly people who have never been there and have never seen anything like that. And they're making wise comments about what it all means. You had to have been there to be able to have any understanding. But they seldom ask veterans who *have* been there to comment.

Morale among Marines in Iraq is high. Maybe it is because they do not listen to the news or read the newspaper. Their news comes to them over the large TV screens in the chow halls, produced by the Department of Defense—an amalgam of BBC, Fox, and CNN. The broadcasts include almost every sports contest in the world. There is a lot of interest in that. Often the din in the chow halls makes it difficult to hear the TV, because most people are sitting together and chatting, ignoring the TV, glad for the few moments of relaxation among their own.

There are no commercials on the Armed Forces Network TV aired in Iraq. That amazing fact dawns on you slowly. There are no ads for spiffy new cars, or thin, made-up women with perfect unblemished faces talking hair color, or bantering about new wireless phone service—no McDonalds Happy Meal ads, no cute animations for cleaning products. The only ads are about military matters—"Think about reenlisting, your country needs you," and "Remember that driving a Humvee is serious business, and the laws of physics apply." Reminders about how grateful everyone at home is for the service of those in Iraq, flashes promoting the news channels, and health reminders—"Don't use snuff"—are part of the upbeat message the military gets. There is Sesame Street, and there are reruns of old sitcoms, as well as newer sitcoms. And there are short feature stories about military personnel doing volunteer work or humanitarian assistance. This is the DoD's version of "clean" TV.

The only place I ever saw the military watching TV for long periods of time was in the waiting room at BIAP. A large wood-floored shack next to the passenger terminal, the waiting room has cots, American electrical outlets all along the walls, and about 100 chairs facing 52-inch TV screens. Military personnel watch their own DVDs on portable compact players, work on laptops, sleep, or veg out in front of the TV. The waits for flights can be long—hours and hours.

In my interviews with the Marine women I never talk about politics, or ask them questions relating to politics. Many times the subject comes up when they ask me questions. A corporal asks me what the phrase "red states and blue states" means. When the subject of political dissension does come up, it is always quickly dismissed with a laugh and something like, "Well, that's why we're here, so you guys back there can have the freedom to argue about anything you want." That is their response—always.

Optimism and pessimism are about neck and neck among the Marines in Iraq. They feel good about the Iraqis they have helped to resettle after the horrendous battles dismantling their cities to get the insurgents out. They feel good about the work they have done in building relationships with the Iraqis as humanitarians and facilitators in building a new, freer society. They are at a loss as to how to get the Iraqi people to settle their differences without violence, and they are not sure the Iraqis will ever be able to learn to trust any leader or any group enough to build a democracy.

When I return to the States, I have a long flight from Kuwait in which to reflect on the extraordinary opportunity to be in Iraq and experience the Marine mission there. I am anxious to get home, but I am disappointed to leave. I realize how exhausted I am from 12- to 16-hour days for more than two weeks of sudden calls for flights on helicopters or rides in Humvees in convoys and yet exhilarated by the morale of all the Marines, especially the women I lived with. Many journalists have embedded with the military for a longer time, and I wonder if they experienced the same bond I developed with "my" Marines. I change planes in London and wander through civilization again—busy people, wrapped up in conversations, eating fast food, talking on cell phones, herding children, absorbed in their own lives. It is a shock. There is no sense of purpose, focus—just aimlessness, no common mission. I find myself wanting to run through the airport yelling, "Hey! There's war in Iraq! Do you care?" That is sheer foolishness. I am embarrassed and get on another flight to continue my ride back to the other world.

I journey for 24 hours over eight time zones, including time in airports en route, changing planes twice. It is like 24 hours between Oz and Kansas. At the airport, early in the morning, my family is there to meet me. I am last coming up from the concourse tram. They are beginning to wonder what has happened.

I am in my own world, wondering if they will be there to greet me, and at the same time wondering what the Marines in Iraq are doing. Glancing at the clock, I feel sad, as one lance corporal had told me. And I know there will be no opportunities for "see-you-laters." I am home and they are in Iraq, a world away. It is very final. Later my children tell me I looked dazed when I appeared at the top of the escalator.

It is several weeks before I can begin to understand why I still feel so close to the Marines in Iraq, why I want to go back. Of course, I would not go back. I am not needed in Iraq. Still, I remember, strongly, the bonds I formed with the women Marines, feeling needed, if only to tell their stories, feeling drawn into their focus. They are interesting, dynamic new friends. We promised to keep in touch. I do not want to lose them. But the world goes on, and eventually I am reconciled to finding that few people are interested to know that I was in Iraq, or why. For a while, I had an immensely important mission. At home, it slowly gets lost in the demands of living, choosing, prioritizing other things.

Many Marines comment to me how pleased they are that I made the effort to come to Iraq and look at the theater in depth, and not just from the point of view of the "shooters" (infantrymen), as many reporters do. They were intrigued that I was there to roam around and see how much work goes into the war behind the scenes—to report the enormous "inside the wire" effort to put the infantry "out there." They tell me I was brave to come. Imagine. For 16 days the Marines sheltered me, transported me, shared meals with me, befriended me, laughed and joked and shared their lives with me. I also shared their awareness of danger and the sense that their morale was high, regardless.

This war in Iraq, politics aside, is a turning point for all women in the military. From the older women Marines who shared their stories of the early years and fought silent battles to build careers as Marines and prove their value to the Corps, to the young women of today who come into the Marine Corps aggressively eager to contribute in the same open manner they would in civilian life, the decision of the Marine Corps to use their skills forward, in a combat zone, has put them all in a position to change forever the acceptance and perception of women as a vital part of the military.

Violence against women continues to be a shadowy part of our culture in the States even as corporate and political, and even religious, ceilings are pierced by more and more women, and more women receive higher education than ever before in our history. Is there violence against women in the Marine Corps? Is there rape? Undoubtedly, but I cannot speak knowledgeably about that as I know of no figures available to measure it. I did not ask that question, and no information about it was volunteered. Is there a lot of sexual activity among the deployed Marines? Of course. Men and women are the same the world over in that respect. But that was not my primary reason for writing about women in the Marines.

After this adventure in the war zone of Iraq, did I learn why women want to be in the Marine Corps? Yes, for the same reasons anyone, a man or a woman, wants to succeed in something that greatly interests them and that encourages success. Now, the U.S. Marine Corps makes it possible for a woman to have as long and as rewarding a career as she chooses. It was not always the case. The culture is different now. As our society has changed its view of women over the years, so has the military.

Still, the military, and in particular the Marine Corps, is vastly different than civilian life. In the Marine Corps, men and women have a mission they share, not just an individual approach to life. They have values in common that they believe in as well as enforce. If this does not work for them, they get out. There is that choice, after they fulfill their initial service requirement. But becoming a Marine changes you. The Marines I interviewed in Iraq told me the things that were important to them, which are the values I have related in this book.

Are those values different than those of male Marines?

As for combat, that debate will be long and convoluted. As long as government officials set that policy, it will be another generation or so before they will accept the inevitability of women in combat. Until there are more veterans of military service to their country among the policy makers, it will not happen. Am I saying it is inevitable? Yes, I think it is. Already the distinction is hazy. Many women have been killed in combat in the Iraq War whether or not they were in a combat unit. Just as all men are not cut out for combat roles, women can determine if they have the right stuff for combat. In this war, women have proven that they can work side by side with their male counterparts and do the job, even under fire, as well as any of the guys. The bond, in most cases, is between Marines, and there is no distinction as to gender.

When you become a Marine, they say, the change is forever. For Marines in harm's way, in Iraq, the bond is forever, as well.

As for how the Marines will handle going back to a world that hardly has an inkling of what they have been through—they hardly think about it. They have more important things to do.

APPENDIX

U.S. MARINE CORPS ABBREVIATIONS OF RANK

Officers in order of rank

Gen	General
LtGen	Lieutenant General
MGen	Major General
BGen	Brigadier General
Col	Colonel
LtCol	Lieutenant Colonel
Maj	Major
Capt	Captain
1stLt	First Lieutenant
2ndLt	Second Lieutenant

Enlisted personnel

SgtMaj	Sergeant Major
MgySgt	Master Gunnery Sergeant
1stSgt	First Sergeant
MSgt	Master Sergeant

GySgt	Gunnery Sergeant
SSgt	Staff Sergeant
Sgt	Sergeant
Cpl	Corporal
LCpl	Lance Corporal
PFC	Private First Class
Pvt	Private

Warrant Officer

CWO5	Chief Warrant Officer 5
CWO4	Chief Warrant Officer 4
CWO3	Chief Warrant Officer 3
CWO2	Chief Warrant Officer 2
WO	Warrant Officer

GLOSSARY

Abaya: A long, flowing gown worn by some Muslim women that covers the entire body except the head and hands. It is often worn with a head scarf.

Abu Ghraib: Location of the infamous prison west of Baghdad.

Aerodrome: Air Base.

Al Anbar: Western-most province of Iraq; under U.S. Marine Corps command.

Al Asad: Iraq's second largest air base, located north of Baghdad.

Al Fajr: Arabic for "New Dawn," the name assigned to the Battle of Fallujah, November 2004.

Al Qaeda: Alliance of militant Muslim guerrillas established by Osama bin Laden.

Al Rasheed: Hotel in the International (Green) Zone of Baghdad.

Baathist: Pertaining to the Baath Party of former Iraqi ruler Saddam Hussein.

Bahrain: Smallest Arab nation, a constitutional monarchy, located on an island in the Persian Gulf.

Billet: Sleeping quarters for troops.

Bird: Slang for helicopter.

Blackwater: Private U.S. firm with contracts to provide security to personnel in Iraq.

Burka: A garment worn by some Muslim women that covers the body completely with mesh across the eyes for vision.

Cammies: Military slang for camouflage clothing.

Chador: Long, full garment worn by Iraqi women, covering the head and body, leaving the face and hands visible.

Chow Hall: Military cafeteria.

Comm: Communications.

Concertina wire: Large coils of barbed or razor wire, which open like an accordion.

Crypto: Cryptography, the encoding of messages for security.

Ditch witch: Construction vehicle for digging ditches.

Fallujah: City in Al Anbar province approximately 40 miles west of Baghdad.

G.I. Bill: 1944 legislation providing educational and other benefits for G.I.s.

Gore-Tex: Patented weatherproof, breathable, outerwear fabric.

Grunts: Marine slang for infantrymen.

Gunny: Slang for Gunnery Sergeant.

Helo: Slang for helicopter.

Hooch: Hut or dwelling.

Huey: UH1 Utility Helicopter.

Humvee: High Mobility Multipurpose Wheeled Vehicle (HMMWV).

Imam: A leader; for Shi'a Muslims, a religious leader.

Inside the wire: On base, inside the concertina wire surrounding the base.

Intel: Intelligence.

Intubated: Tubes inserted in a human body for medical treatment.

Ipso Facto: Latin for "in and by the very fact."

Jihadist: One who literally "struggles in God's way," often using violent warfare.

Kevlar: Brand name for very light, very strong synthetic fiber used as body armor.

Kuwait: A country, a constitutional monarchy, on the southeastern border of Iraq.

Logistics: The framework of operations in the military organizing transport, storage, and construction.

Master Guns: Master Gunnery Sergeant.

Mecca: The holiest city of Islam, located on the west coast of Saudi Arabia.

Medivac: Medical evacuation.

Mosul: Iraq's second largest city, about 250 miles north of Baghdad.

Mujahideen: Also called Muj—Muslim guerrilla warriors engaged in Jihadi warfare.

Oorah: Spirited yell used by Marines (not to be confused with the Army's "Hooah").

Outside the wire: Outside the concertina wire delineating the parameters of military bases.

Pax sticks: Passenger flights.

Per diem: Latin for "by the day"—expenses paid for special duty, travel, etc.

Portapotties: Portable toilets.

Psyops: Psychological operations.

Quonset: Lightweight, prefabricated corrugated steel structure with semicircular ends.

Rack: Military slang for bed or cot.

Rear: Military bases in the United States; sometimes used to mean inside the wire.

Rhino bus: Heavily armored vehicles with V-shaped undersides to deflect bomb blasts.

Route Irish: Highway from the Green Zone to Baghdad International Airport.

Samarra: City approximately 80 miles north of Baghdad.

Semper Fi: Short for Semper Fidelis—Always Faithful—the Marine Corps motto.

Sharia: The body of Islamic law meaning "the way" or "path."

Sheik: Tribal elder, leader, or scholar—a revered person.

Shia: Also Shi'a—a denomination of Muslims who split from the Sunnis 14 centuries ago.

Solatia: Payments of money for solace, consolation, or comfort.

Spartan: Characterized by austerity, discipline, and self-denial—after the ancient Greek state of Sparta.

Sunni: Muslims who make up the largest denomination of Islam.

Taqqadum: Iraq's largest air base, approximately 115 miles west of Baghdad; now a U.S. Marine air base.

Yemen: Arab country, a parliamentary republic, on the southwest tip of the Arabian Peninsula.

INDEX

ABOUT THE AUTHOR

SARA SHELDON is the director of Boulder's Leanin' Tree Museum of Western Art, a freelance writer, and author of *Operation Restore America* (1998). Her research for this work was conducted while she was embedded with the 1st Marine Expeditionary Force in Iraq.